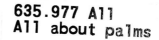

ORTHO® ALL ABOUT

Palms

DISCARD

Meredith® Books
Des Moines, Iowa

Ortho All About Palms
Editor: Denny Schrock
Contributing Writer: Paul Craft
Contributing Photographers: Paul Craft, Ed Gohlich
Copy Chief: Terri Fredrickson
Copy Editor: Kevin Cox
Publishing Operations Manager: Karen Schirm
Senior Editor, Asset and Information Management: Phillip Morgan
Edit and Design Production Coordinator: Mary Lee Gavin
Art and Editorial Sourcing Coordinator: Jackie Swartz
Editorial Assistant: Susan Ferguson
Book Production Managers: Pam Kvitne, Marjorie J. Schenkelberg, Mark Weaver
Imaging Center Operator: Chris Sprague
Contributing Copy Editor: Susan Lang
Contributing Technical Proofreaders: Timothy K. Broschat, Scott Zona
Contributing Proofreaders: Fern Bradley, Susan Brown, Barb Rothfus
Contributing Indexer: Ellen Sherron
Other Contributors: Janet Anderson, Quail Botanical Garden

Additional Editorial Contributions from Art Rep Services
Director: Chip Nadeau
Designers: lk Design

Meredith® Books
Editor in Chief: Gregory H. Kayko
Executive Director, Design: Matt Strelecki
Managing Editor: Amy Tincher-Durik
Executive Editor: Benjamin W. Allen
Senior Associate Design Director: Tom Wegner
Marketing Product Manager: Brent Wiersma

Executive Director, Marketing and New Business: Kevin Kacere
Director, Marketing and Publicity: Amy Nichols
Executive Director, Sales: Ken Zagor
Director, Operations: George A. Susral
Director, Production: Douglas M. Johnston
Business Director: Janice Croat

Senior Vice President: Karla Jeffries
Vice President and General Manager: Douglas J. Guendel

Meredith Publishing Group
President: Jack Griffin
Executive Vice President: Doug Olson

Meredith Corporation
Chairman of the Board: William T. Kerr
President and Chief Executive Officer: Stephen M. Lacy

In Memoriam: E.T. Meredith III (1933–2003)

Photographers
Photographers credited may retain copyright © to the listed photographs. L=Left, T=Top

Clemson Univ. - USDA CES, Bugwood.org: 45TL

All of us at Meredith® Books are dedicated to providing you with the information and ideas you need to enhance your home and garden. We welcome your comments and suggestions about this book. Write to us at:
Meredith Corporation
Meredith Gardening Books
1716 Locust St.
Des Moines, IA 50309-3023

If you would like more information on other Ortho products, call 800/225-2883 or visit us at: www.ortho.com

Note to the Readers: Due to differing conditions, tools, and individual skills, Meredith Corporation assumes no responsibility for any damages, injuries suffered, or losses incurred as a result of following the information published in this book. Before beginning any project, review the instructions carefully, and if any doubts or questions remain, consult local experts or authorities. Because codes and regulations vary greatly, you always should check with authorities to ensure that your project complies with all applicable local codes and regulations. Always read and observe all of the safety precautions provided by manufacturers of any tools, equipment, or supplies, and follow all accepted safety procedures.

CONTENTS

PALM PRIMER

Nothing evokes an image of the tropics more vividly than a palm. A coconut palm with leaves swaying in a tropical breeze on a beach silhouetted by a colorful sunset is a selling tool for vacation getaways worldwide. Palms symbolize the tropics, but they are not exclusively tropical. Many of the 2,500 palm species tolerate cooler climates where temperatures occasionally drop below freezing. Some can handle temperatures in the teens or colder for a short time. The sight of a snow-covered windmill palm shouldn't surprise anyone— that palm's native habitat is the foothills of the Himalayan Mountains.

Palms are native throughout the world in tropical, subtropical, and temperate areas. Their heights range from 1 to 300 feet. They may have a single trunk, form a clump of multiple trunks, or develop a vining growth habit. Palm leaves are feather or fan shape, and some are covered in spines. Bluish leaves, red new growth, reddish trunks, and colorful fruit and flowers make certain palms quite colorful at times.

When first described by botanists, palms were called principes of the plant kingdom. The word principes, Latin for prince, is a name that palm fanciers recognize as a synonym for palms. Palms lend grace and regality to the landscape, which is reflected in palm names such as royal palm, king palm, majesty palm, queen palm, and princess palm.

Fossil records indicate that palms have existed for roughly 70 million years. While other plant families such as cycads have been around for as long as 230 million years, palms have a long history of flourishing, while cycads have dwindled to a few oddity species today. New species of palms are still being discovered, and species once thought extinct are being rediscovered.

Some interesting palm trivia includes the following: Coco de mer palm bears the plant kingdom's largest seed, weighing as much as 50 pounds; raffia palm has the world's largest leaf, measuring 80 feet long; rattan palms are the source of all rattan furniture; and vegetable ivory palm produces seeds from which buttons and carvings are made rivaling those fashioned from elephant ivory.

▶ **This Mediterranean-style home has a formal entry courtyard graced by elegant palms. Large featherlike fronds provide some shade for the tiered fountain surrounded by blooming plants.**

PALM MORPHOLOGY

Flowering plants are divided into two major groups: monocots and dicots. The seedlings of monocots emerging from the ground have one leaf, while those of dicots have two leaves. Palms, grasses, orchids, bromeliads, lilies, and bamboos are monocots. Dicots include woody ornamentals such as oaks, maples, and leafy shrubs, and many herbaceous perennials such as daisies, geraniums, petunias, and marigolds.

The tissue inside the plant stem is arranged differently in monocots and dicots. If you look at a cross section of the trunk of a woody dicot, you can see annual growth rings of the trunk with an outer cambium layer (region from which new bark and wood develop). The xylem (water-conducting tissue) and phloem (food-conducting tissue) that make up the vascular system are adjacent to this cambium layer in a uniform ring.

If you look at a cross section of a palm, you can see these tissues in the form of vascular bundles, which look like small dots, scattered through the cross section of the trunk. The trunk of a palm tree does not expand with annual growth rings as it ages. A palm is unable to heal itself when its trunk is injured, whereas in a dicot the cambium layer gradually grows over and seals off the injury.

The growing point of a palm is called the heart, also known as the apical meristem. It is located near the top of the trunk and ties in with the vascular system. Leaves are produced in this heart. If you were to cut it open, you would see leaves in all stages of development down to the center of the palm heart. Once the heart is cut through, however, the palm dies because it cannot produce another one.

▲ A cross section of palm (above) shows scattered vascular bundles. A dicot hardwood log cross section (below) shows annual vascular rings and bark on the surface.

▶ Some palms such as this fishtail palm have variegated foliage.

▲ The flowers of Norfolk Island palm develop into reddish brown fruits.

Root growth in monocots such as palms also differs from that in dicots. A palm has no taproot. Instead an area at the base of the trunk is called the root initiation zone. The roots continuously grow from this region, and they stay the same diameter throughout the life of the root.

Palm flowers grow on flower clusters that emerge either below or among the leaves. Some species of palm have male and female flowers on the same branch. Others produce all male or all female flower branches intermittently. Still other palm species have separate male and female plants. Monocarpic palms produce a single massive flower cluster at the end of their lives.

The ripe fruit of many palm species often contrasts colorfully with the foliage: It can be yellow, white, deep red, purple, or black. It also ranges in size from smaller than a pea to as much as 50 pounds. The fruit usually contains one seed, but in some species may bear two to four seeds held tightly together. The seeds have a hard shell (endocarp) that protects the embryo and endosperm, the food source for the embryo when it germinates. Generally only one sprout comes from each seed.

▲ Coco de mer palms produce the world's largest seeds. This one is nearly a foot long.

PALM LEAF TYPES

P alms can be categorized into one of three basic leaf types.

Fan-leaf palms Fan-leaf palms have palmate leaves, which are shaped like a fan or the palm and outstretched fingers of a hand. The leaf stem is attached close to the center of the leaf and the segments radiate out from that center point. Depending on the palm species the segments radiate completely around the center point, creating a circular leaf, or they radiate only partially around the center, creating a V shape. The leaf segments of most fan palms are divided part way to the center or sometimes nearly to the center point. In a few species, such as ruffled fan palm, the segments are joined together nearly to the segment tips creating a solid leaf. Costapalmate palms are a subcategory; they have a short midrib instead of a center point from which the leaf segments radiate.

Feather-leaf palms Feather-leaf, or pinnate, palms have leaves that resemble a feather. The leaf stem, also known as the rachis, extends nearly the entire length of the leaf. The leaflets are attached at intervals in two rows on opposite sides of the leaf stem. If single leaflets are spaced along each side, the leaf appears to be flat. In some species, multiple leaflets are joined at a single point on the leaf stem and radiate out at different angles, giving these palms an especially feathery appearance. Crownshaft palms are a subset of feather palms; they have leaf bases that wrap around the top part of the palm trunk creating a sheath or collar. The sheath can be as short as 1 to 2 inches long or up to 4 or 5 feet in length. Crownshaft palms tend to shed leaves cleanly, leaving a smooth trunk.

▲ **Chinese fan palm has palmate leaves. Its partially divided segments radiate from a single point at the base of the leaf.**

◀ **A majesty palm frond is an example of a feather-leaf, or pinnate, palm. Leaflets are attached in rows on opposite sides of the leaf stem.**

Bipinnate palms These palms have a secondary leaf stem that is attached to the primary one, and the leaflets are connected to the secondary stem at regular intervals. The various fishtail palms—species of *Caryota*—are the only bipinnate palm. Their leaves appear triangular when viewed from a distance.

◀ **Fishtail palms have bipinnate leaves. Leaflets extend from the main leaf stem in pairs much like a feather-leaf palm, but the leaflets are divided, creating a series of fan shapes along the secondary leaf stem.**

IDENTIFYING PALMS

Although the word "taxonomy" can be intimidating, it refers to a relatively simple science for identifying all plants, including palms. The various parts of the plant are examined in progression to key the plant by genus and species. Space limitations prevent providing a key for all palms in this book, but describing some of the characteristics to look for will help you understand how the process works based on the palms listed in the palm gallery beginning on page 50.

First look at the leaf shape. Does it belong to a fan-leaf, feather-leaf, or bipinnate palm? If the answer is bipinnate, then you're looking at a fishtail palm—a species of *Caryota*. If the answer is feather-leaf palm, check to see if the plant has a crownshaft. If it does, is the crownshaft long or short? Long crownshaft palms include the palms in the chart below. Short

crownshaft feather-leaf palms include *Heterospathe, Pseudophoenix,* and some species of *Chamaedorea* and *Dypsis.* If your feather-leaf palm has no crownshaft but has spines on the trunk or leaves, it's one of the palms listed in the middle section below. Feather-leaf palms with no crownshaft and no spines are the ones listed in the bottom section below.

To determine which species your palm belongs to, divide each group by the type of bloom. Are male and female flowers on the same branch, or are male and female flowers borne separately on bracts of the same plant, or on separate male and female plants? The size of the mature plant is also helpful in determining species as is knowing whether the emerging leaves are a colorful red or not. Fruit and flower colors are also helpful in identifying a palm.

Fan-leaf palms can be keyed similarly.

FEATHER-LEAF PALM SPECIES OF VARIOUS CROWNSHAFT TYPES

FEATHER-LEAF PALMS WITH LONG CROWNSHAFT

Adonidia	Dictyosperma	Pinanga
Archontophoenix	Drymophloeus	Ptychosperma
Areca	Dypsis (some)	Rhopalostylis
Carpentaria	Euterpe	Roystonea
Carpoxylon	Hydriastele	Satakentia
Chamaedorea (some)	Hyophorbe	Veitchia
Chambeyronia	Kentiopsis	Wodyetia
Clinostigma	Neoveitchia	
Cyrtostachys	Normanbya	

FEATHER-LEAF PALMS WITH SHORT CROWNSHAFT

Chamaedorea (some)	Heterospathe
Dypsis (some)	Pseudophoenix (left)

FEATHER-LEAF PALMS WITH NO CROWNSHAFT BUT WITH SPINES

Acrocomia	Calamus	Phoenix
Aiphanes	Desmoncus	Salacca
Astrocaryum	Metroxylon	Verschafeltia
Bactris	Pigafetta	

FEATHER-LEAF PALMS WITH NO CROWNSHAFT AND NO SPINES

Allagoptera	Elaeis	Parajubaea
Arenga	Gaussia	Pelagodoxa
Asterogyne	Geonoma	Phytelephas
Attalea	Howea	Raphia
Beccariophoenix	Jubaea	Ravenea
Butia	Laccospadix	Reinhardtia
Calyptrocalyx	Lytocaryum	Rhapis
Calyptrogyne	Marojejya	Syagrus
Ceroxylon	Nypa	Wallichia
Chamaedorea	Orania	
Cocos	Oraniopsis	

LIGHT REQUIREMENTS

The diversity of the palms includes species that prefer full sun as well as ones that grow best in deep shade. Tall canopy palms characteristically need full sun while smaller species—often with unique features—grow in shade. Some are emergent species, meaning that they prefer shade when young and then grow better in full sun as they mature.

Avoid planting palms that prefer full sun all their lives in heavy shade. Their leaves will stretch and their trunks will be thin as a result of low light. Grown in shade these palms will never be robust, and in time they will die.

Growing shade-loving palms in full sun does not work well either. The leaves of palms that are adapted to low light will burn in bright light. The foliage will turn brown and die.

If in doubt about the light requirements of a palm you'd like to grow, refer to the gallery starting on page 50.

Some palms that grow best in 50 percent shade or more (heavy shade) include those in the list at bottom right.

Some palms do equally well in light shade or in full sun—after growing the first few years of their life in shade. They include the palms listed below.

▲ Chinese fan palm growing in too much shade stretches toward the light and develops thin foliage.

▲ Shade-loving parlor palm develops sunburned foliage when it grows in an area with too much sun.

Scrutinize the light in the area where you want to plant a palm. Make sure the palm you place there will do well in the available light. With the wide variety of palms to choose from, you should have little difficulty in finding a suitable one for the situation.

PALMS FOR LIGHT SHADE OR FULL SUN

Arikury palm	Ruffle palm
Betel nut palm	Sagisi palm
Bismarck palm (below)	Salak palm
Dwarf sugar palm	Saw palmetto
Formosa palm	Seashore palm
Lipstick palm	Spiny licuala
Peach palm	Stilt root palm
Pygmy date palm	Yahanna palm
Red feather palm	

PALMS FOR HEAVY SHADE

Atherton palm	Hollrung palm	Polaris palm
Baby coconut palm	Hooker's fishtail palm	Rat's tail palm
Beguine palm	Ivory crownshaft palm	Ravimbe palm
Bougainville palm	Joey palm	Tiger palm
Cat palm (above)	Mapu palm	Tuna tail palm
Cauqui palm	Miniature fishtail palm	Vegetable ivory palm
Chontilla palm	Parlor palm	Velvet palm
Flame palm	Pinanga caesia	Windowpane palm

TEMPERATURE REQUIREMENTS

Palms come from many different climate zones, and the range of temperatures that they have adapted to is extreme. Some species originated in lowland areas that are hot year-round. In these locales the air cools slightly at night, but still remains warm. Daytime highs are often 95°F or higher, while nighttime lows seldom dip below 78°F. Palms from mountainous regions may see daytime highs in the 70s or 80s, and nighttime lows in the 40s and 50s. Some species such as windmill palm occasionally experience snow in their natural habitat. Mexican blue and Guadalupe palms brave summertime temperatures exceeding 100°F in parts of Mexico.

Some palm species can tolerate a wide range of temperatures, and others cannot. Most species from mountainous or temperate climates cannot withstand the summer heat of South Florida. Likewise lowland Amazon species tend to do poorly in California. Most of the problem can be traced to nighttime lows. California cools off more at night than Florida. Species accustomed to higher temperatures at night fare better in Florida, while palms that prefer cooler nights do better in California. Taking into account the temperatures your area experiences year-round will help determine which species of palms will grow best for you.

▲ **Palms adapted to the Florida Keys must tolerate high nighttime temperatures as well as high humidity.**

PALMS ADAPTED TO COOL NIGHTS

Andean wax palm	Miniature Chusan palm
Atherton palm	Nikau palm
Blue needle palm	Norfolk Island palm
Bronze palm	Purple king palm
Chilean wine palm	Quito coconut palm
Kentia palm	Sentry palm
Manambe palm	Spiny fiber palm

PALMS ADAPTED TO WARM NIGHTS

*Açai palm	*Lipstick palm	Spindle palm
Australian licuala	Mexican astrocaryum	*Stilt root palm
Beguine palm	Orange collar palm	Sunshine palm
*Betel nut palm	Peach palm	Talipot palm
Bottle palm	*Pinanga caesia	Three anther palm
Bougainville palm	*Polaris palm	*Tiger palm
Carpentaria palm	Raffia palm	Unleito palm
*Chontilla palm	Sagisi palm	*Vegetable ivory palm
Coconut palm	*Salak palm	*Wanga palm
Fishtail lawyer cane	*Samoan palm	*Windowpane palm
*Hollrung palm	Silver star palm	*Yahanna palm
*Ivory nut palm	Solitaire palm	Zombie palm

* Best where temperatures stay moderate year-round as in Hawaii.

◄ **Although summer daytime temperatures may be quite hot in interior California, nighttime temperatures generally are much cooler. Palms adapted to this climate must also tolerate dry conditions.**

SOIL REQUIREMENTS

Acid versus alkaline soil

Soil pH ranges from acidic ones, such as those found on the volcanic islands of Hawaii, to the alkaline limestone soils in extreme South Florida. Many palms tolerate a wide range of pH and do well in either acidic or alkaline soil. Other species prefer one or the other. Planting an acid-loving palm in alkaline soil almost guarantees that the plant will not thrive. In addition to pH tolerance, an important soil requirement for almost all palms is good drainage, regardless of whether a species prefers wet or dry conditions.

Serpentine soil

Some soils that palms grow in are highly unusual. Serpentine soils found in parts of Cuba and New Caledonia have an extremely high concentration of magnesium and iron. The soil often contains levels of other elements such as nickel and cobalt that would ordinarily be toxic to plants. These places are often left uncultivated because crops won't grow there. But some species of palms thrive in such soil. Each serpentine area has a unique combination of potentially toxic minerals, and palms from these areas do not always adapt to the soil found in home landscapes. They may be extremely difficult to grow outside their natural range. However old man palm, miraguama palm, and some species from New Caledonia adapt well to ordinary garden soil.

▶ Queen palm is an acid-loving palm that will develop foliar discoloration if grown in alkaline soil.

PALMS FOR ACIDIC SOIL

Assai palm	Hooker's fishtail palm	Purple king palm
Atherton palm	Joey palm	Queen palm
Australian licuala	King palm	Rat's tail palm
Baby coconut palm	Lipstick palm	Ravimbe palm
Black palm	Madagascan palm	Stilt root palm
Bougainville palm	Mapu palm	Sunset palm
Flame palm	Piccabeen palm	Tiger palm
Foxtail palm	Pinanga caesia	Windowpane palm

▶ Old man palm grows in serpentine soil in its native Cuba, but adapts well to most well-drained garden soils.

PALMS FOR ALKALINE SOIL

Bailey palm
Barbados palm
Blue latan palm
Borhidi palm
Bottle palm
Buccaneer palm
Canary Island date palm (pictured)
Chinese needle palm
Cuban petticoat palm
Cuban wax palm
Date palm
Key thatch palm
Maya palm
Miraguama palm
Seashore palm
Silver thatch palm
Spindle palm
Tuna tail palm
Velvet palm

MOISTURE REQUIREMENTS

DROUGHT-TOLERANT PALMS

Arikury palm
Blue hesper palm
Blue needle palm
Buccaneer palm
Canary Island date palm (pictured)
Date palm
Desert fan palm
European fan palm
Gingerbread palm
Key thatch palm
Licury palm
Mazari palm
Pindo palm
Saw palmetto
Seashore palm
Silver thatch palm
Thatch palm
Triangle palm

Palms vary greatly in the amount of moisture they require. Some species are at home in a desert oasis, while others thrive along streams where they are periodically inundated by water. Majesty palm could even be considered semiaquatic; it grows along flood-prone streams in Madagascar. The vast majority of palm species fall somewhere between the extremes in moisture needs. No matter what moisture conditions are present in your garden, you can likely find an appropriate palm species that will tolerate

▲ **Blue hesper palm grows well in full sun on this rocky, dry hillside.**

those conditions quite well. Consult the list below left to find palms that prefer wet conditions or the list above for those that prefer dry sites.

Irrigation

Both drought-tolerant and moisture-loving palms grow well when given the proper amount of water. All palms thrive with year-round moisture provided either by rainfall or irrigation. Some palms require water once a week, while others prefer it two to five times a week. When designing your landscape think about the water demands of your plants and then place palms with similar water demands together so they can be watered uniformly. Mixing palms that have different watering requirements makes it difficult for all species to thrive. Excess water can cause rot, and too little water can lead to wilting. In either case certain palms in the mixed planting will thrive and others will not.

If you have an automatic irrigation system, create zones that can be watered separately and incorporate palm species with similar water needs within those zones. The same is true if you hand water. Trying to hand water a moisture-loving palm in the midst of drought-loving plants will spread too much water to those that do not want it.

PALMS TOLERANT OF MOIST TO WET CONDITIONS

Açai palm
Assai palm
Australian licuala
Black sugar palm
Carpentaria palm
Ivory nut palm
King palm
Lipstick palm (pictured)
Majesty palm
Mangrove palm
Mexican fan palm
Needle palm
Paurotis palm
Raffia palm
Redneck palm
Royal palm
Sago palm
Salak palm
Vonitra palm
Wanga palm

USES OF PALMS

In terms of use by humans, palms are the second most important family of plants on earth after grains. Palms in one form or another affect the lives of almost everyone on the planet. Their uses include food, building materials, and various household products.

■ **Food** Coconut, Chilean wine, and gru-gru palms are a small sampling of the many palms that provide tasty seeds. Fruit from such palms as date, peach, and pindo are eaten fresh or turned into jellies. Juice from the fruit of açai palm is touted for its health benefits. Palm hearts from many species, especially assai palm, are harvested and eaten either fresh or canned. (Because the heart is the growing part of the palm, harvesting it kills the palm.) Sap is collected from the cut flower bracts of toddy fishtail palm and turned into an alcoholic drink. The center pith from the trunk of sago palm is processed into edible starch.

▲ **Palm hearts are a tropical delicacy.**

▲ **The flower branches of pacaya palm are used as food in some regions.**

■ **Shelter** Leaves from many palms including Belize thatch, chontilla, cohune, caranday, and coconut palms are used for long-lasting roofing thatch, which is still commonly used on houses throughout the tropics. Coconut palm leaves are also woven into room dividers. The trunks of palms are used as building timbers and fence posts, and they are split for house siding and flooring. Coconut wood makes durable flooring sold throughout the world. In the Caribbean, house siding made from royal palm trunks lasts for decades.

■ **Products** Rattan furniture, which is used worldwide, comes from rattan palms such as fishtail lawyer cane. Brooms are made from leaf fibers of various species of *Coccothrinax*. Hats are fashioned from the leaves and fiber from several palm species such as coconut palm and *Coccothrinax*.

▲ **Thatch made of palm fronds is a common roofing material in the tropics.**

▲ **Hats and bags may be made from palm leaf fibers.**

Handbags made from the leaves of silver thatch palm are popular in the Dominican Republic. The seeds from vegetable ivory palm, similar in texture and hardness to elephant ivory, are used to make buttons and various ornamental carvings. Plantations of African oil palm produce palm oil, which is used in foods and as light machine oil as well as a biofuel. Shredded coconut coir—fibers from the nut's husk—is used as a renewable peat substitute in potting mixes.

▶ **Rattan furniture is popular for casual settings.**

▶ **Coir—shredded coconut husk fibers—makes a good water absorbant soil amendment.**

DESIGNING WITH PALMS

▼ The smooth crownshafts of purple king palms are a vertical accent in this landscape, and the large fronds provide shade for sago palms, blue agapanthus, pink impatiens, and snake plant.

Before purchasing any palms, develop a landscape design to help you visualize the end result. Measure existing features in your landscape and the spaces between them. Mark out those distances to scale on paper. If you have plants already in the ground, add them into your drawing. Research the palms you like and determine if their sizes are appropriate for the areas you are considering. Talk to nursery or landscape professionals to get their thoughts and ideas. Envision the palm species you are contemplating to see if they fit the style of your garden. Think about the other plants you have or want to incorporate along with the palms so you can develop an overall idea of how they will work together. If there's a neighboring property you want to screen or a feature you wish to highlight as a focal point, note them. Doing your homework before the first shovel goes into the ground increases your chances of ending up with the result you want.

In this chapter you will learn how to use palms in the landscape. Palms can cast shade, provide screening, cover the ground, or vine into tree canopies. Their enormous size range provides the option of using palms of whatever dimensions you need for any landscape situation. They can be the dominating theme of the landscape or serve as a small accent. Palms work as solitary specimens, in small groupings, or as a canopy grove. Combine species to offer strikingly different appearances and create drama in the garden. When paired with other plants many palms become standouts. Other palms are better suited as a backdrop for plants with a unique form or dazzling color. Palms are adaptable to either formal or informal landscapes. Use them in the garden to create a unique landscape theme. As container plants around pools, decks, and porches, they are unequaled.

For centuries palms have proved themselves to be among the best indoor plants. Whether grown in individual pots, large planters, or in a conservatory, they offer beauty and gracefulness unlike any other plants. Just as you do outdoors, combine other indoor plants with palms to enhance the beauty of both.

Use palms as much or as little as your creativity dictates. No matter how you use them, palms will serve important functions in your garden and home. First consider their growth habits so you will know how to make the best use of them.

GROWTH HABITS OF PALMS

Palms can be classified according to one of four growth habits: tree, shrub, groundcover, or vine. Here are descriptions and examples of palms belonging to these categories.

▶ **Coconut palm is an example of a treelike palm with a single trunk.**

▼ **Areca palm develops into a large shrub with multiple stems.**

▶ **Miniature fishtail palm makes an attractive groundcover.**

◀ **Fishtail lawyer cane clambers through the canopy of tall trees.**

▼ **Hooks on the leaf of fishtail lawyer cane enable it to climb.**

Tree

Tree palms have a single trunk. In gardens the largest types can grow up to 100 feet tall with a leafy top that spreads 25 feet or wider. The trunk diameter can be up to 5 feet. Other types may grow to only 6 feet tall with a 3- to 4-foot spread and a trunk diameter of an inch. While large trees such as coconut, royal, and Samoan palms provide canopy and shade, small ones such as bougainville, cauqui, and tuna tail palms grow in the shade of larger trees and provide ornamental appeal on a smaller scale. Gingerbread palm branches freely, eventually creating a canopy up to 40 feet across.

Shrub

Shrubby palms are those that clump and produce multiple trunks. These clustering species can range from just a few feet tall to 30 feet or more. Some create dense clumps that completely block a view, while others are more open. Some such as areca, cat, and lipstick palms make excellent screening plants or hedges. Others including blue needle, flame, and three anther palm make superb focal points in the landscape.

Groundcover

These low growers are single- or multitrunk palms that reach a maximum height of 4 feet. They include miniature fishtail, mapu, and velvet palms. Use multiple plants of the same palm under taller palms or woody plants to create a mass planting. Palms that work as groundcovers are shade-lovers and cannot be grown in full sun. A single groundcover palm properly placed can also make an unexpected little focal point in a small space.

Vine

More than 300 species of lawyer canes (*Calamus*) and several other palms are vinelike. They may be single or multitrunked. The tallest grow as much as 300 feet up through tree canopies. Some are quite ornamental and make good conversation pieces. Long, whiplike projections called cirruses protrude from the end of each leaf. The cirrus is a modified leaflet armed with backward hooks or spines to assist the palm in grabbing onto a tree trunk to pull itself up through the tree canopy. The palm's pliable stems are the source of rattan furniture.

LANDSCAPE USES OF PALMS

With so many species and growth forms, palms can be used in a multitude of ways. They offer a canopy for shade, act as privacy screening, or serve as an accent or focal point. Some grow best in hot sun, while others thrive in dark shady areas. Dry sandy or rocky conditions suit certain species, and wet conditions are better for others. Some palms grow well when exposed to the salt air of the ocean, and others are intolerant of salt. There's a palm to handle just about any landscape situation that arises.

Scale

Because palms range dramatically in size, one of the first considerations when designing a landscape is to choose palms that are in proper scale with their surroundings. Avoid using palms that are massive or grow extremely tall near a small house or on a small lot. A Canary Island date palm that is five to six stories tall with a crown 25 feet across is completely out of scale near a single-story 1,200-square-foot house on a 75-foot-wide lot. The palm becomes the focus of attention, dwarfing the small home. Nikau palm, which does not become as big, is a better choice.

The opposite problem develops if you use a lone 6-foot-tall pygmy date palm in front of a large two-story house. The little palm will look lost as a solitary planting, but can be effective if planted with larger palms to complement the scale of the house.

▲ Keep in mind the ultimate size of the palms you plant. These palms dwarf the one-story home that they shade.

▶ Lady palm develops a dense canopy that serves as a visual barrier or screen.

Creating a canopy

Palms can make a wonderful shady canopy. Picture coconut palms along a tropical beach with a hammock strung between two of them. If you can grow coconut palm, try recreating that same effect in your own landscape. (Space the palms approximately 12 to 15 feet apart to accommodate a hammock.)

Canopy palms are fast to moderate growers capable of creating shade across a diameter of 15 to 20 feet or more. For a more naturalistic feeling, plant palms of varying heights at random distances. Some species that work well to create this effect are kentia, king, overtop, queen, sagisi, Samoan, and sunshine palms.

If you plant two palms close together they will bend away from each other as they grow, creating a graceful arch. After a palm canopy is established, you can plant shade-tolerant plants underneath.

Privacy screening

Palms are seldom considered for hedges or privacy screens, but some species are well suited to these uses. Areca palm has long been utilized as a hedge or screen in South Florida. Many other multitrunk palms work well, too. Cat palm creates excellent screening. See the list at right for other palms that are good screening candidates. They do not need to be used as a single species in a long row. Mix leaf types and species for a more casual appearance.

ACCENT PALMS FOR SHADE

Atherton palm
Baby coconut palm
Beguine palm
Cauqui palm
Chontilla palm
Dwarf lady palm
Elegant palm
Joey palm
Mapu palm
Needle palm
Pacaya palm
Polaris palm
Tiger palm
Velvet palm

◀ A grove of royal palms creates a shady haven.

PALMS FOR PRIVACY

Blue needle palm
Cabada palm
Farihazo palm
Formosa palm
Ivory cane palm
Ivovowo palm
Lady palm
Lipstick palm
Macarthur palm
Paurotis palm
Seashore palm
Spiny licuala
Three anther palm

▶ **Sunshine palms of varying heights create a naturalistic grouping.**

▲ **Several palm leaf types and colors combine in this entryway planting to welcome visitors.**

SMALLER ACCENT PALMS

Blue latan palm
Bottle palm
Cuban wax palm
Formosa palm
Lipstick palm
Manila palm
Pindo palm
Red feather palm
Satake palm
Spindle palm
Stilt root palm
Traveler's palm
Yahanna palm

LARGE ACCENT PALMS

African oil palm
Bailey palm
Bismarck palm
Canary Island
     date palm
Chilean wine
     palm
Cohune palm
Cusi palm
Date palm
Ivory nut palm
Ronier palm
Silver date palm

▶ **Palms in containers form the backbone of this tropical poolside grouping of plants.**

Accents

If you want to create a focal point in your landscape, consider large palms that have a dramatic effect, such as those in the list below left. If you want a subtler effect or if the space requires a smaller species, try one of the palms in the list of small accent palms above left. Use any of these palms in groupings of three or more to enhance the dramatic effect, or tie the entire landscape together by spreading them throughout the yard.

Instead of arranging single-trunk palms in a grouping in which the plants appear separate, you could focus more attention on the palms by planting them close together so they look as if they arise from one root zone. For the most pleasing appearance use odd rather than even numbers of plants in a group. The list at right indicates some palms adapted to cluster planting.

Mixing leaf types

One way to add flair to your landscape is to mix fan palms with feather palms. A grouping of sagisi palms with several smaller ruffled fan palms underneath is a delightful combination, as is kentia palm with Chinese needle palm planted beneath.

You can plant large fan palms close to large feather palms for more visual interest.

Container palms in the landscape

Many palms are attractive in containers around pools and on patios and porches. The same light, temperature, soil, and moisture requirements apply to container palms as they do to landscape palms. Fast growing plants outgrow containers quickly, so choose slow-growing palms, which should be able to remain in the same container for two to four years. After that time repot them into a larger container.

PALMS FOR CLUSTER PLANTING

Betel nut palm
Black palm
Carpentaria palm
Carpoxylon palm
Coccothrinax spp.
Coconut palm

Foxtail palm
Guadalupe palm
Howea spp.
Princess palm
Pygmy date palm
Royal palm

COMBINING PALMS WITH OTHER PLANTS

Informal or formal

Palms lend themselves to informal use in the garden, and they're perfect for creating a casual tropical atmosphere. A naturalistic landscape with curving lines and blending of harmonious plants is the essence of an informal tropical garden.

Palms are also well suited to the formal garden, which is characterized by symmetry, straight lines, and squared-off hedges. They offer an element of grace and elegance to such a landscape. Paired palms with straight trunks and full crowns equally spaced fit the formal garden extremely well. Palms are unrivaled when used to soften the corners of buildings or emphasize entrances. They can make handsome framing elements on opposite sides of hardscape features in the garden such as pools and patios.

A cat palm hedge never needs trimming to maintain a constant height, density, and dark green color. A driveway lined on both sides with royal palm trees is like a cathedral.

Using other plants with palms

Use broadleaf and needled trees, shrubs, and groundcovers with palms to show off all elements of the landscape. A landscape consisting of only palms can be beautiful, but palms combine well with other plants. While a grove of coconut or kentia palms can be stunning, a mixed canopy of palms with other woody plants creates a more natural display reminiscent of the palm's native habitat.

Numerous woody and herbaceous plants add texture and color to a garden. Some of these plants are focal points and others serve as wonderful fillers that enhance the palm they accompany.

Anthurium, elephant ear (Alocasia), and philodendron have unique leaf shapes and colors that complement palms. Choose from the many species and cultivars available. Some are vines that grow up the trunks of palms and add a different perspective to the garden. Gingers and heliconias add unique flowers and foliage; they make a scenic backdrop for an accent palm. Bromeliads have unique flowers that contribute color to the landscape, and some sport colorful leaves as well. They make excellent groundcovers or accent plants under the canopy of a palm. Ferns of many shapes and sizes add softness to the

An allée of date palms underplanted with citrus trees creates a dramatic formal appearance in this garden.

landscape. Tree ferns are accent plants in their own right, and many lower-growing ferns make attractive groundcovers. Ornamental grasses such as muhly or fakahatchee grass are first-rate choices for mass planting under tall palms. They provide a naturalistic feel to the garden. Spathoglottis ground orchids make superb groundcover plants or small accents around palms in the landscape.

Cycads are often confused with palms, partially because their common names often include "palm", and because their leaves resemble palm fronds, but they belong to a different plant family. A mass planting of coontie or cardboard palm under a grouping of coconut palms, fan-leaf palms, or palmettos is simply gorgeous.

A mass of bromeliad foliage brightens the ground under this blue hesper palm.

▶ Various palms, cypress, and New Zealand flax combine with modern architecture to provide this California landscape with a distinctly regional appearance.

Broadleaf canopy trees are ideal for creating shelter for shade-loving palms. The broad leaves make a dense canopy in which low-light palms thrive. Tall shade palms—such as açai, assai, kentia, ruffle, and silver star—will produce a secondary canopy under the tree. Small palms—including Chinese needle, flame, mapu, parlor, polaris, and rat's tail—can be planted underneath.

Golden trumpet (*Allamanda*), bougainvillea, angel's trumpet

▶ The palms at the end of this pool and patio area create a privacy buffer.

(*Brugmansia*), yesterday-today-and-tomorrow (*Brunfelsia*), gardenia, flame of the woods (*Ixora*), Bangkok rose (*Mussaenda*), and rhododendrons are among the many flowering shrubs and vines that look great under or around palms. The brightly colored foliage of croton and cordyline provides year-round color. Use the blooms and foliage as a strategically placed splash of color.

Landscape buffers

Although palms can create an excellent screen or hedge on their own, you can develop a more dramatic landscape buffer by using other foliage or flowering plants in conjunction with palms. Strive for a layered look that adds color and different leaf textures.

A recipe for a spectacular buffer starts with multitrunk palms of different leaf types. Add a few single-trunk palms for extra height and texture. To get a denser planting place tall heliconias behind parts of the buffer. Heliconias add a wonderful leaf texture and flowers; use several different species to take advantage of their unusual flowers. Locate philodendrons such as giant philodendron, 'Rojo Congo', and 'Xanadu' in front. Tuck in bird's nest anthurium here and there for even more variety. Throw in some spiral ginger, red button ginger, and variegated shell ginger for their unique flowers. Include a pinch of brightly colored ti plant and you will have a visually stunning tropical buffer.

Cordyline and cycads combine well with palms in theme gardens.

Dense layers of plantings in several levels create a rain forest appearance.

This palm at the edge of a vanishing pool makes a picturesque silhouette against the distant hills and sky.

Theme gardens

A theme garden uses plants from a certain region to create the ambience of that locale. To make a Caribbean garden, choose palms native to that area such as buccaneer, cabbage, Cuban wax, gru-gru, Maya, royal, silver thatch, thatch, and zombie palms. Complement the palms with anthurium, bougainvillea, coontie, gumbo-limbo *(Bursera)*, oak *(Quercus)*, paradise tree *(Simarouba)*, philodendron, plumeria, and other plants found in the Caribbean.

Another example of a theme garden is a South Seas garden planted with carpoxylon, coconut, Fiji fan, princess, red feather, ruffled fan, and Samoan palms. Various cordylines, elephant ears *(Alocasia)*, gingers, and wood ferns *(Dryopteris)* are just a few of the associated plants to include in your South Seas landscape.

A rain forest-theme garden is an example of plants that come from a particular type of growing environment rather than a specific region. If you prefer to be less specific, create a tropical theme garden using plants with a tropical appearance and similar growth requirements regardless of area of origin.

A theme narrows down the possible list of plants, but at the same time it lets you create a unique garden. Plants that are native to one region generally have similar soil, water, fertilizer, and temperature requirements, which makes maintenance easy. If the architecture of your home fits a particular part of the world where palms grow, match the landscape to that style of architecture to create an even more striking effect.

Palms surrounding a water feature double your viewing pleasure with their reflected images in still water.

Ferns add texture and clivia and scarlet sage provide brilliant color in this rain forest planting that uses palms as a backdrop.

PALMS INDOORS

For centuries palms have been prized as indoor plants. They hold up better indoors than most other plants and they add a lushness and feel of the tropics. Many species have proved how adaptable they are to growing indoors. For a palm species to do well there, it must tolerate low light and dry air. Kentia and lady palms are among the best species for indoor use. Also good choices are many species of *Chamaedorea* including bamboo, cauqui, dwarf bamboo, hardy bamboo, miniature fishtail, pacaya, parlor, and velvet palms. Other palms that succeed indoors are arikury, baby coconut, curly kentia, pygmy date, ruffled fan and sagisi palms. Although areca, Chinese fan, clumping fishtail, and majesty palms are commonly used as potted plants, they hold up less favorably; they need more light and humidity than is usually provided indoors, and may need to be replaced after a year.

Large palms such as foxtail, macarthur, Manila, Mexican fan, queen, solitaire, and thatch palms have been used effectively in large indoor planters in shopping malls and office buildings. However, they are too large to use in most homes.

Types of use

The most common indoor use of palms is as potted plants. They add color and softness to home and office interiors.

▲ Croton, parlor palm, and pygmy date palm make a bold statement in this living room grouping of potted houseplants.

On a larger scale, palms can be added to big planters built into homes, office buildings, and malls. Skylights, which are often placed above these planters, provide the plants with natural light. Irrigation lines and drains are usually built in to make maintenance easier. The size of the planters provides the opportunity to combine palms with a variety of other plants. Larger palms—and more species of them—can grow successfully in spacious planters because their root growth is less restricted than in individual pots.

The ultimate indoor use of palms is in a conservatory, which typically is temperature-controlled and has a fan to circulate the air. It may also have misters to create the higher humidity that indoor plants like. The conservatory may re-create a specific outdoor environment in which the chosen palm can thrive. It could duplicate the environment of the steamy tropics or it may resemble a slightly cooler mountainous climate. Home conservatories reached peak popularity in Victorian times but have become fashionable again in recent years.

◀ With adequate light indoors even large palms can thrive in shopping malls, hotel lobbies, and office buildings.

Indoor humidity is often low; air-conditioning and heat dry the air dramatically. Because most palms come from humid areas, adding humidity to the air is usually beneficial. Misting your plants with water is of little benefit. It is better to use a room humidifier or cluster several plants together to raise the humidity. Or grow palms in a bright bathroom where steamy showers add moisture to the air.

Light

Palms need light to survive, and natural light is best. If your home doesn't have a window with a bright exposure or a skylight, then your palm will need supplemental lighting. Many kinds of systems are available. Grow lights, which closely mimic the spectrum of natural light, promote excellent growth but may be expensive. Regular fluorescent lights provide much of the light spectrum needed by plants and are relatively inexpensive to purchase and operate. Incandescent light is usually unsatisfactory as a supplemental light source because it wastes a lot of energy in the form of heat rather than light. But supplemental incandescent light is better than no light at all. Whatever system you choose, provide a minimum of 8 to 10 hours of supplemental light per day.

Moisture

Indoor light levels, temperatures, and humidity levels all affect the rate at which the soil in plant containers dries out. As a result each indoor situation is different, but generally soil doesn't dry out as fast indoors as it does outdoors. Most palms need to be watered only when the soil becomes nearly dry to the touch. Stick your finger an inch or so into the soil. If the soil feels cool and moist, wait to water until it is drier. Add water until it seeps out of the drain holes into a saucer under the pot. Let the pot drain for a half hour and then dump the excess water from the saucer.

▲ Pygmy date palm, China doll *(Radermachera)*, and majesty palm add formal elegance to this living room.

CARING FOR INDOOR PALMS

▲ Brown leaf tips are a sign of low humidity, improper watering, or excess salts in the soil.

▲ This container full with several butterfly palms will soon need repotting.

Repotting

A palm growing in a container will eventually need to be repotted. The potting mix gradually breaks down and the palm's roots become restricted. Under such conditions the palm declines. Slow-growing and small species can remain in the same container for two to four years. After that repot the palm into the next larger size pot using a well-drained potting soil with little organic matter, such as Miracle-Gro® Cactus, Palm & Citrus Potting Mix. A mix of 50 percent peat moss and 50 percent perlite or coarse sand also works well. If the palm has outgrown its interior space, consider transplanting it into your garden.

Fertilizing

Potted palms require a different feeding program than palms grown in the ground. A continuous-feed fertilizer such as Osmocote™ provides nutrients for your container plant for 6 to 9 months. Use a balanced (nearly equal amounts of nitrogen, phosphorus, and potassium) liquid fertilizer on occasion to maintain deep green foliage. Avoid overfeeding because fertilizer salts may build up in the soil and cause leaf burn. Counteract fertilizer build-up by leaching out these salts. (Flush the potting mix with pure water to wash the excess fertilizer away.)

Growing conditions indoors are not as favorable to palms as conditions outdoors. Consider rotating two identical palms periodically between an indoor location and a protected porch or patio. The period outdoors will help rejuvenate the palm and keep it in top shape for display indoors.

Diagnosing problems

Most problems with palms grown indoors can be traced to inadequate light or insufficient moisture. If the leaflets of your palm develop brown tips that steadily become browner, the problem lies in the root system. Brown leaf tips are usually caused by overwatering, underwatering, low humidity, or excess fertilizer. The key to helping the plant recover is to determine the specific cause.

Sometimes soil that is dry on top can be soggy in the bottom of the container. Roots suffocate in excessively wet soil and die back. On the other hand, roots dry out and die when soil moisture is inadequate. Check the dampness of the soil through the entire rooting zone of the container. A moisture meter may be helpful in determining when to water.

When palm leaves appear washed out and pale, the cause might be too little light. Move the plant to a brighter spot. If that is not possible, provide supplemental light.

Spider mites are the most common indoor insect pest of palms; they are favored by dry conditions with little air circulation. If you notice yellow stippling on the leaves, look more closely for fine webbing or moving dots on the leaf undersides. Because spider mites are tiny, a hand lens will more readily help you see them. Wash the leaves with a damp rag or apply a forceful spray of water to remove the pests. Insecticidal soap spray is also effective in controlling spider mites. To prevent a reinfestation increase the humidity around your palm and give it an occasional shower to wash off the mites.

INDOOR PALM PLACEMENT

The most important consideration in placing palms indoors is to provide sufficient light. Bright natural light from a window or skylight is best. A sunroom, conservatory, or greenhouse is ideal. If you wish to put the palm in a dark corner, provide supplemental light for at least 8 to 10 hours a day. By using supplemental light you can place palms wherever they best fit your decorating scheme.

Containers

The various lady and bamboo palms can be used as specimens, screens, or room dividers because they form spreading clumps. Baby coconut, kentia, and ruffled fan palms as well as many species of *Chamaedorea* make good floor plants. For indoor use they are often sold with three plants in one container to add fullness to the planting. Palms are available in all sizes to fit whatever height your decor needs. If your home has high ceilings, a tall plant such as kentia palm is an excellent candidate. Arikury, pacaya, and thatch palm also work well in this situation. Purchase these palms large enough to be in scale with the space. Make certain that they have been acclimated for indoor use.

Miniature fishtail and velvet palm are ideal for use on a tabletop. You may find them sold individually or as multiples in a single pot. Choose the form that fits the look you want to achieve and the space in which you intend to place them.

Consider combining multiple containers of palms in an area. Mixing heights and leaf textures can create a dramatic effect. Use an odd number of plants for the best effect. Virtually all palms that grow well indoors combine well with one other. Mix in anthuriums, philodendrons, and other common indoor tropicals for the unique forms and textures they provide.

Indoor planters

Essentially a large container that can hold multiple plants, an indoor planter permits you to plant tall and short palms together. Ruffled fan palm underplanted with miniature fishtail palm is a beautiful combination. Bamboo palm planted in an elongated planter works perfectly as a screen or room divider. As with container plants and landscape groupings, combine the palms with other compatible plants to create a pleasing design.

▲ The pool next to this palm adds needed humidity to the air.

▲ A single fan palm in a container spreads to fill a wide space.

▲ Fishtail palms combine with dracaenas, blooming bromeliads, and philodendrons in this shopping mall planter. A skylight provides adequate light to ensure healthy growth.

Conservatories

A conservatory could be considered the ultimate planter. Because it provides good light and humidity, and also lets you easily control watering needs, the major limitation is the height to which palms will grow. Palms cannot survive being cut back; top pruning removes their growing point. Therefore, choose slow-growing and small species that will not exceed the height of the conservatory.

For best growth use a well-drained potting soil mix in which the palms and other plants you're growing will thrive. In the controlled environment of a conservatory plants grow well and will crowd each other if there are too many plants. Exercise restraint and consider the ultimate size of your palms and companion plants. Use only a few large species to provide a canopy. Underplant the canopy palms with several plants of medium height, and add groundcover species to complete the look.

BUYING, GROWING & CARING FOR PALMS

PURCHASING PALMS

When picking a palm for your landscape follow some simple guidelines to be sure you select one that will be suitable for your situation and intended purpose.

■ **Site conditions** Become familiar with the conditions where the palm will be planted.

■ Is the soil wet or dry?

■ Will the area get regular irrigation?

■ Is the soil acidic or alkaline?

■ Is the site sunny or shady? During what times of day does it receive sun or shade?

■ Is the planting spot windy?

■ How do you intend to use the palm? For example, are you trying to create a focal point, shade an area, create a backdrop, or block a view?

■ Do you want a palm that will stay small, or grow tall and spread out?

> When shopping for a palm, slide the plant out of its pot. A healthy palm has vigorous white or tan roots.

▼ This healthy old man palm has excellent deep green frond color.

After answering these questions you will be better prepared to find the proper palm for your conditions.

■ **Grower experience** Find a grower or nursery with a good reputation. Knowledgeable growers will be much more helpful in finding the right palm for your intended use and growing conditions. They should be able to answer your questions easily, and their plants should be properly identified and labeled.

■ **Plant quality** Look for a palm that is insect free and has good color and healthy foliage—no spots, no brown tips, and no stunting or malformations. The plant shouldn't look thin and stretched out. It also should be well rooted and not wiggle

easily in its pot. Conversely the roots should not circle the pot or be growing out the drainage holes.

■ **Nursery conditions** Ask what conditions the plant was grown in. Depending on its species, each palm prefers full sun, deep shade, or something in between. Even if the plant is a sun lover, it may have been grown in some shade. In such a case the palm may sunburn if you plant it in full sun right away. You can overcome the problem by gradually moving the palm into increasing amounts of sunlight before actually planting it.

Impulse buying can create problems that have a major impact on your landscape. That adorable little palm you see in the nursery may seem ideal for the small space between a garage and a walkway, but it may grow into a giant-size palm. Plant your palm in a place it can grow into, not a place it will grow out of.

> The yellow-green fronds and brown leaf tips of this old man palm indicate that it has been stressed. It is not a suitable plant to purchase.

PLANTING CONTAINER-GROWN PALMS

Time of year to plant

Depending on where you live, when you plant a palm may be important. In Hawaii and South Florida, palms can be planted year-round. However, avoid planting during a lengthy dry season because watering a new palm can be an issue. Until a palm becomes established, it needs regular water or it may suffer irreparable damage. If regular irrigation is unavailable, wait to plant until wetter weather returns.

If you live where winter brings freezing or near-freezing temperatures, wait for warmer spring weather. Newly planted palms are more sensitive to low temperatures than established plants and are more apt to suffer cold damage. Roots establish more slowly in cold weather than they do in warm weather, another reason to pick a warm season for planting.

Picking the location

Your palm may prefer a particularly wet or dry location. Consider planting it in a low area (unless it is a tender palm planted in a frost-prone area) or close to a sprinkler if it likes wet conditions. Palms that prefer drier conditions may do better on a berm.

Make sure that your palm has adequate room to grow. Mark the location where you intend to plant the palm and then stand back to imagine what it will look like when it's full grown. Measure the area to be sure the palm won't be cramped by structures or other plants as it grows. Watch the sun throughout the day to be sure the amount of light is sufficient, and think about how the light in that area will change as other plants around the palm grow. Also keep in mind the palm's rate of growth in deciding if this location is the right one.

Digging the hole

Excavating a planting hole may seem simple enough, but depending on where you live it could be a major undertaking. The limestone rock in extreme South Florida or the lava rock in the Hawaiian Islands can make digging even a small hole difficult. Clay soils in California and other locations can also be very compacted and hard to dig. Regardless of soil type, dig a hole at least twice as wide as the diameter of the root ball of your new palm, and make the hole no deeper than the root ball. Loose soil under the root ball will settle after planting, creating a poorly drained depression around the palm. Although these guidelines are not as important where soils are looser or sandy, it is still a good idea to follow them.

Planting

Exercise care in handling your new palm. While some species tolerate rough handling, many do not. The heart, the area from which all the leaves grow, can be delicate in some species. If the palm is shaken or bounced up and down during the ride back from the nursery, this growing area can crack or shatter. The damage may not become apparent for days or weeks afterward, but in severe cases the palm could die or its growth could be browned or stunted.

When you remove the container from the root ball, be careful to minimize damage to the roots. Some palms do not take kindly to having their roots cut or bent and will undergo severe shock. You may find it easier to cut the container away from the root ball than to try to pull it off.

Plant the palm so that the bottom of its trunk, where the roots emerge, is flush with the soil level in the garden. Sometimes a palm will push up in its container, exposing the upper part of its roots. Be sure to cover these roots with soil when you plant the palm. And if the palm was buried a bit deep in its container raise the root ball when you're planting so that the trunk is at the proper depth.

Backfill the planting hole with loose soil. The loose soil will make it easier for the roots to grow and for the palm to become established. Roots grow into rocky or hard clay soils with difficulty. Ideally the loose soil should drain well and be similar to the surrounding soil. If your soil is lava rock, a finer grade of lava cinders is a good backfill. If your soil is limestone rock, you could use coarse sand. If you have hard clay soil, loosen the soil as much as you can by breaking up large clods. You can

---

SOIL AMENDMENTS

Several universities have done studies about the benefits of amending planting soil. Their conclusions are that amending the soil may be of little benefit and may cause problems later on. Adding rich organic soil, peat moss, or other organic amendments may seem like the proper thing to do, but the plant's roots tend to stay within the amended soil and not venture out into the surrounding soil. The planting hole acts like a container that restricts development of the plant later on. Ask your nursery professional if the plant you purchased for your location is an exception to this rule.

also add organic matter such as compost throughout a planting bed to help loosen the clay. Avoid amending the backfill soil only with organic matter. The developing roots will be less likely to expand beyond the planting hole in such a case.

Avoid compacting the backfill. Once the soil is at the proper level, place the palm in the center of the hole and check to be sure it is at the proper depth. Make adjustments if necessary. Backfill more loose soil around the root ball, and water the root zone thoroughly, making sure there are no air pockets under or around the root ball. Roots that come in contact with an air pocket will cease to grow and die.

Once you've thoroughly watered in the palm, make a small soil dam on the soil surface around the outside of the root ball. Add water inside the dam on a regular basis to direct the water down into the root zone. This is especially important for palms planted on slopes.

PLANTING A PALM

▲ This 45-gallon containerized bismarck palm is ready to be planted.

▲ Make the hole at least twice as wide as the root ball.

▲ Slide the palm out of its container. You may need the help of a friend or a professional landscaper.

▲ An abundance of firm healthy roots indicate that this palm is in good condition for transplanting.

▲ Measure the depth of the hole to make certain the excavation is the correct depth.

▲ Center the root ball in the hole with the top of the root ball at or slightly above the level of the surrounding soil.

▲ Backfill around the root ball with existing top soil.

▲ Form a soil ring slightly wider than the root ball to hold water.

▲ With regular care this properly planted bismarck palm will thrive.

PLANTING FIELD-GROWN PALMS

▲ Dig a wide hole to create a zone of loose soil for new roots to grow into. The wider the hole the easier it will be for the transplanted palm to become established.

▶ Place the root ball on a firm soil base. Make certain that the roots will not be exposed above the soil line or buried too deeply.

Field-grown palms may be dug up by hand or by a machine such as a tree spade. Handle field-grown palms or those that are being transplanted from another in-ground location in much the same way as container-grown palms. The main difference is that the field-grown palms have had their roots cut when dug and thus have a smaller root mass to absorb water. They will need to regenerate new roots to reestablish themselves. Their initial water requirement is greater than that of container-grown palms whose roots have not been severed. Water them more frequently and with a greater amount of water at each watering until new roots regenerate.

Field-grown palms may also lose some of their older leaves when transplanted. The leaves turn yellow and then brown and drop. When a palm cannot draw enough water from its severed roots, it sacrifices some of its older leaves in favor of supporting new growth.

Exercise the same care in handling and planting a field-grown palm as you would a container-grown specimen. It is even more critical to plant field-grown palms in consistently warm weather when the roots will reestablish more rapidly. The root balls of field-grown plants are often more irregular than those of container-grown palms; when watering them in be sure to remove air pockets from around the root ball. Because they require more water than transplanted container-grown palms, make the soil dam around them larger than the root ball. Fill this reservoir with water and allow the water to seep down into the root zone, where it is needed most.

STAKING PALMS

Container-grown palms rarely need staking because their root balls are intact and big enough to hold the palm upright. Field-grown palms, however, often have small root balls in proportion to their height. In such cases the palms are top heavy and can topple during wind storms if left unsupported.

The best way to support a palm is to brace it rather than tie it to a stake. Because palm trunks are often smooth, ties used in staking can slip down the trunk. Bracing is much more effective. Three or four braces of 2×4 lumber equally spaced around the palm are sufficient. Make them long enough and place their bottom ends far enough from the palm to allow support in strong winds. To fasten these braces to the palm, fashion a collar around the trunk. Wrap burlap around the trunk at the appropriate height to protect the trunk from scratches or scrapes, and then secure an equal number of small pieces of wood around the collar with metal bands or a similar tie that will not permit the wood to slip up or down the palm during high winds. Securely nail the braces into the small pieces of wood. Never nail directly into the palm because the wounds would never heal and they would create an entry point for insects and diseases. At the bottom of each brace, insert a 2×4 stake into the ground that the brace can be nailed into. Leave the braces in place for one year or until the palm has reestablished sufficient roots to stay anchored on its own.

▲ Pad the trunk of a braced palm to protect it from damage by the supports. Here wood braces are held in place with metal bands to prevent the braces from slipping out of place.

▲ Recently transplanted palms may need bracing to prevent them from toppling in strong winds. The large fronds of foxtail palm are likely to catch the wind and uproot the tree until new roots develop.

CARING FOR NEW PLANTINGS

▲ Mulching a planting bed is a good way to conserve moisture and reduce weed problems at the same time.

▲ Sunburned palm foliage bleaches yellowish green then turns brown. Underwatering a new planting compounds the problem.

A newly planted palm provides clues when environmental conditions are not to its liking. Watch for brown leaf tips or older leaves that turn yellow and die before they should; excess fertilizer and improper watering are possible causes. A sun-loving palm may have been grown in shade, and its leaves can sunburn if you plant the palm in full light right away without gradually exposing the plant to increasing amounts of sunlight. Correcting the cause of such problems will help a palm recover quickly.

Initial feeding

The palm you purchase from a garden center or nursery likely has been fertilized well. Let the plant acclimate to your garden before feeding it again. Two to four weeks after planting, apply a palm fertilizer. For most palms a complete fertilizer with two parts nitrogen, one part phosphorus, and three parts potassium along with one part of magnesium is ideal. Fertilize again after another month or according to the directions on the product label. After the palm is established fertilize four times a year as explained in more detail on page 35.

Newly planted palms that are no longer restrained by a container initially grow a vigorous root system, which in turn supports more top growth. Horticultural professionals often provide extra phosphorus during the initial month or two after transplanting to promote root growth, but the practice is controversial because excess phosphorus is not good for the environment and research has failed to demonstrate any benefit to root growth from the additional phosphorus. Use products such as triple superphosphate (0-45-0) judiciously. It leaches into the ground, so broadcast it around the palm where the developing roots can absorb the leached phosphate.

Watering

During its first year a transplanted palm forms more roots than normal to establish itself in the landscape. Some additional watering during this phase provides for the plant's needs until its roots spread to collect water from a wider area. But too much water may discourage roots from spreading and delay the palm's progress.

The root structure of container-grown palms remain intact, so watering three or four times a week is sufficient for most species; moisture-loving palms need more frequent watering. During unusually hot or dry weather give new plantings extra water.

A ring of mulch several inches deep around the base of this newly planted majesty palm reduces competition from grass for moisture and protects the trunk from damage by a lawn mower or string trimmer.

Field-grown palms may require daily watering. Water in the morning and again in the evening on particularly hot and dry days. After three to four weeks gradually cut back on watering to four or five times a week for another three to four weeks. Then reduce your watering schedule to three or four times a week.

If a palm's lower leaves turn yellow and brown, that could be a sign it's not receiving enough water. The problem is more likely to occur on field-grown palms rather than container-grown palms. Correct the problem by giving the palm more water. On the other hand if the soil does not drain well and stays wet between waterings, a palm's roots can rot. Take steps to improve the drainage, apply water less frequently or do both.

Mulching

Use mulch around the base of a palm to help the soil retain moisture and to keep out weeds. As the mulch breaks

down it provides an enriched organic soil amendment around the palm. Apply only a 2- to 4-inch-deep layer of mulch; make the layer thinner near the trunk and thicker over the root zone. Excess mulch piled against the trunk can cause rot and fungal disease in the trunk and prevents water from penetrating into the root zone.

Mulch is a better groundcover around your palm than lawn, which uses up moisture and nutrients intended for the palm. The lawn also creates a maintenance problem when it needs trimming close to the palm. Never use a string trimmer around palms because the string can cut and permanently scar the trunk.

Controlling weeds

Use weed control products such as glyphosate (Roundup) around your new palm with caution. Some palm species are more sensitive to herbicides than others. The palm can suffer damage if the herbicide comes in contact with green stems, foliage, or exposed roots. Symptoms of damage include brown leaf spots, browning foliage, deformed new growth, and, in extreme cases, death. It is better to hand pull weeds around your new palm until it becomes established.

The lower leaves of this newly planted majesty palm are turning brown, which is an indication that it may be underwatered.

CARING FOR ESTABLISHED PLANTINGS

Watering

■ **Know your palm** The palm gallery, beginning on page 50, includes a description of the water requirement for each palm. The various palms are described as drought-tolerant, or having low, moderate, or wet watering needs. Several are aquatic, meaning that they can grow with their roots submerged in water. The key on page 51 tells you how often to water for each of these classifications.

Premature browning of leaves or leaf tips can be a sign of too much or not enough water. Feel the soil around the plant to determine whether it's wetter or drier than the plant needs.

■ **Know your soil** A water-loving palm planted in fast-draining soil needs watering more often than one planted in soil that drains more slowly. The ideal soil for palms contains about 50 percent water holding material such as compost and 50 percent porous material such as sand. Palms need good drainage, even if they prefer a lot of moisture. Poorly drained soil limits the amount of oxygen available to the roots causing them to suffocate and die.

To determine whether your soil drains adequately, dig a hole approximately a foot deep and wide and fill it with water. If you have a hard time filling the hole because the water continuously pours through, your soil drains excessively fast. If the water takes several hours to disappear, your drainage is poor. But if the water fills easily and takes just 15 to 30 minutes to soak in, then your drainage is good.

■ **Duration of watering** It is better to water less often but for a longer period each time than it is to water more often but for a shorter period. When you water for

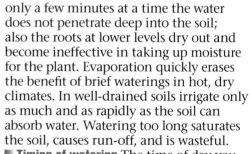

▲ **Miracle-Gro® Shake 'n Feed Continuous Release Palm Plant Food includes the micronutrients that palms need.**

only a few minutes at a time the water does not penetrate deep into the soil; also the roots at lower levels dry out and become ineffective in taking up moisture for the plant. Evaporation quickly erases the benefit of brief waterings in hot, dry climates. In well-drained soils irrigate only as much and as rapidly as the soil can absorb water. Watering too long saturates the soil, causes run-off, and is wasteful.

■ **Timing of watering** The time of day you water is important. Watering during the heat of the day means much of the water is wasted as it evaporates into the atmosphere. The best time to irrigate is in early morning just before sunrise so the water has a chance to percolate down into the soil and benefit the plant.

◀ **Test the drainage of your garden soil by digging a hole and filling it with water. The longer it takes for the water to drain, the poorer the drainage of your soil.**

▲ Yellow-orange spots on older palm leaves are one indication of potassium deficiency.

▲ **Nitrogen deficiency**

▲ **Potassium deficiency**

▲ **Magnesium deficiency**

▲ **Manganese deficiency**

▲ **Iron deficiency**

▲ Apply fertilizer uniformly over the root zone of the palm. For established palms this means spreading the fertilizer from the trunk all the way out to the drip line (extent of branch tips).

Feeding

■ **Fertilizer formula** Provide the right combination of nutrients for your palms to yield healthy, robust plants. Research from the University of Florida indicates that potassium is the most important element in a palm's diet. Nitrogen and magnesium are also needed in relatively large amounts. The micronutrients manganese and iron are important too. Phosphorus, which is required by most plants in large amounts, is relatively unimportant in palm nutrition. The end result is a recommended formula containing nitrogen, phosphate, and potash, with magnesium and micronutrients. It is critical that the nitrogen, potassium, and magnesium in the fertilizer be in a slow-release form. If the nutrients are released too quickly, the root system can absorb only a portion of them. The rest are wasted and potentially pollute the environment.

Apply the slow-release fertilizer every three months (four times per year). Although low winter temperatures reduce a plant's ability to take up fertilizer, soil temperatures remain more moderate than air temperatures and root growth remains active longer than top growth. The best way to apply the fertilizer is to broadcast it around the entire root zone of the plant. The palm fertilizer formula also works well for other landscape plants so it is all right to broadcast it throughout your garden.

■ **Nutrient deficiencies** Insufficient amounts of each nutrient cause characteristic symptoms to develop, usually in the foliage. Following are descriptions of the most common nutrient deficiency symptoms in palms.

■ **Nitrogen** This deficiency shows up as general yellowing of the leaves. Treat it with the palm fertilizer described above, or you can apply a liquid foliar feed such as Miracle-Gro® LiquaFeed.

■ **Potassium** Look for yellow spotting in the older leaves, which in severe cases can spread to the youngest leaves. Apply slow-release potash (0-0-34) with magnesium to correct the problem. (The reason for including magnesium is to prevent magnesium deficiency, which could occur because of the additional potassium.) It may take a palm up to two years to recover completely from potassium deficiency because it has to produce new leaves to replace all the affected ones.

■ **Magnesium** Identify this deficiency by bright yellow appearing on the leaflet tips and extending toward the leaf stem on older leaves. Eventually the newer leaves are affected as well. Prilled kieserite is an excellent slow-release source of magnesium to correct the problem.

■ **Manganese** Also called frizzletop, manganese deficiency generally shows up on acid-loving palms grown in alkaline soils. The newest growth emerges deformed with dead, brown areas. The condition worsens if left untreated. Apply manganese sulfate to the soil or spray it on the leaves to cure the deficiency. Avoid planting acid-loving palms in alkaline soil.

■ **Iron** You can recognize iron deficiency by yellowish leaves with green veining. The newer leaves are affected first. This deficiency is sometimes associated with palms that are planted too deep or planted in waterlogged soil. If either is the case, remedy the situation before beginning treatment. Use a chelated iron compound; EDDHA is the most effective one in alkaline soils.

▼ **A pole saw is helpful for reaching into the palm canopy to remove dead leaves.**

▼ **A sharp pruning saw is needed to remove large leaf stems.**

▼ **A hand pruner is an effective tool for trimming small palms.**

Pruning

Pruning palms is far simpler than pruning other woody ornamentals. All you have to remove are dead leaves and old fruit stems. Crownshaft palms make it easier still; they shed leaves that have turned brown. Pick up the dropped leaves and compost or dispose of them.

■ **Pruning equipment** The tools used for trimming palms are likewise simple. Hand pruners work well for small palms; a pruning saw is better for larger ones. Use a pole saw to remove dead leaves on tall palms. When the palm grows taller than the reach of a pole saw, decide how important dead leaf removal is to you. All palms eventually shed their old leaves, and the petticoat of dead leaves can become an ornamental feature in tall palms.

But if you want the dead leaves removed from tall palms, you have two options, both involving professional assistance. The first option is to use a cherry picker, a hydraulic lift with a basket on the end in which the tree trimmer stands. The lift hoists the trimmer to the crown of the palm so that it can be pruned. Renting a cherry picker can be expensive, and the reach of the lift may be inadequate for extremely tall palms. The second option is to hire a tree climber who will climb the palm to trim off old leaves. The disadvantage of this option is that most tree climbers use boots with metal spurs. They climb by driving these spurs into the trunk as they ascend, in the process injuring the palm and sometimes leaving unsightly holes that become permanent features. The holes also provide entry points for diseases and insects.

■ **When to prune** The best course is to remove palm leaves only after they have turned completely brown. As the old leaf dies it translocates nutrients to the newer leaves. By cutting off leaves that retain some green, you are robbing the tree of these nutrients. In addition, as long as the leaf has some green in it, it can photosynthesize and produce new food for the tree. Repeated removal of green leaves can lead to pencil pointing, a condition in which the trunk becomes narrower and narrower at the top where the leaf crown forms. The leaves become smaller as well. If excessive trimming continues the palm may never regain its health. However, partially green or yellow leaves can be quite unsightly. You can safely remove dying leaves when they are more than 50 percent brown with few long-term consequences to the tree.

■ **Pruning techniques** Throughout coastal areas untrained tree trimmers conduct hurricane trimming, a technique that is detrimental to palms. The practice has gone on for so long that many homeowners don't realize that it harms the plant. Many palms are quite wind-resistant. They are not damaged by high winds nearly as severely as broadleaf woody trees. Yet the myth persists that cutting most of the leaves from a palm helps it survive a hurricane. The opposite is true. Severe trimming weakens the crown to the point that it may snap off even in moderate winds. Severe pruning also stresses the tree, making it more susceptible to diseases and insect infestations.

If you want to prune a palm in preparation for a hurricane, trim off only those leaves that hang below the horizontal

⬆ This sabal palm is in need of pruning. Older leaves are brown and dying, detracting from the plant's appearance.

◀ After proper pruning the palm still looks healthy and full, but no longer has unattractive leaves. In addition leaf removal improves the view.

◀ These coconut palms have been trimmed excessively. The few remaining fronds will not provide enough energy for the trees to thrive.

◀ You can sterilize pruning tools to avoid spreading diseases by swabbing them with rubbing alcohol between each cut.

plane of the crown. This practice retains a sufficient leaf crown to maintain the health of the palm. More severe trimming can injure the palm. Allow the palm to grow a complete ball-shape crown before pruning it again.

It is also particularly important to feed pruned palms regularly. The added nutrients guarantee adequate nutrition to the palm to compensate for nutrients removed by pruning.

When removing a leaf, cut it as close to the trunk as possible. The remaining leaf base eventually falls off, but it may take several years, and if you try to strip the leaf base from the trunk before it is ready to fall off, you can scar the trunk. In some species such as date palms, you can create an interesting pattern on the trunk by cutting the leaf stems at a uniform distance from the trunk.

To help prevent the spread of diseases such as fusarium wilt, treat your pruning tools with isopropyl alcohol or hydrogen peroxide after you finish pruning one palm. Dip or swab your hand pruners and saw in either of these undiluted liquids to sterilize the cutting surface.

WINTER PROTECTION

◄ **Foxtail palm shows freeze damage to its foliage. New growth may be unaffected as long as the heart remains above freezing, but the browning of frost-damaged leaves will be permanent.**

alm species vary greatly in their sensitivity to cold. Some species tolerate temperatures in the high teens for short periods, while others are damaged when temperatures dip below 45°F. For the best results plant only palms that are hardy to the normal minimum winter temperature in your area. Trying to grow palms that are too cold-sensitive for your garden can be an exercise in frustration. For those occasions when temperatures dip below normal and put your palms at risk, you can take preventive steps to minimize damage.

Preventing cold damage

One of the best ways to protect a cold-sensitive palm is to plant it in a warm microclimate, such as behind a windbreak or in a sheltered courtyard, to protect it from the chill of cold winter winds. Planting under a canopy can also be beneficial because warm air rises and the canopy keeps some of that air from escaping. Cold air settles and flows through lower areas of the landscape—so another way to protect palms is to avoid planting them in low spots or at the base of a hill.

Protecting potted palms

Take potted palms into the house, garage, porch, or other covered area during a cold snap. If the potted palm is too large or too heavy to move, follow these recommendations for protecting them.

▲ **Windmill palm is one of the most cold-hardy species. It can withstand hard freezes.**

◄ **You can provide several degrees of frost protection for your palm by draping a lightweight blanket or sheet over it.**

Covering palms

Prior to the cold snap cover your palms with sheets, blankets, or burlap to protect them from cold as well as frost damage. Don't use plastic sheeting because condensation develops inside the plastic and freezes when it gets cold. Any foliage that touches the plastic will be damaged. Cloth insulates better than plastic, and condensation is less likely on cloth. Be sure to cover the entire plant. Allow the cover to drape loosely over the palm so that warm air rising from the soil will be trapped under the cover, keeping the plant inside warmer than the outside air. This method keeps the plant 4 or 5 degrees warmer than outside air during brief cold dips.

Using heaters

Heat from a propane barbeque grill placed near a cold-sensitive palm can help protect it from the cold. Other types of propane heaters may also be effective. Use a fan to blow the warm air toward the palm. Keep the heater far enough away from the palm to prevent overheating or burning. Provide constant surveillance to prevent possible mishaps. If high winds are associated with the cold, propane heaters may prove ineffective. Electric space heaters are not recommended because they are dangerous to use outdoors.

Watering for frost protection

Water the soil around the palm prior to a cold snap. Moist soil stays warm longer during a cold snap because water loses heat less rapidly than dry soil. Take care to keep water off the plant: When water freezes on the plant, it causes damage to the plant tissues below.

Farmers and orchardists run overhead irrigation to protect crops from cold. As ice forms on the plants the water releases heat. By continuing to irrigate, the farmer can maintain the plant temperature at a constant 32°F. However, winds associated with the cold can cause the ice to become colder. A possible consequence of this

▷ **For warding off the chill of temporary cold spells a propane heater placed near frost-sensitive palms may provide the necessary protection.**

▽ **Palms planted at the top of a slope will be less likely to suffer freeze injury because cold air will flow to the base of the hill.**

method of protection is leaf and stem breakage from the weight of ice.

Frost protection from overhead sprinkler irrigation is impractical in most home landscapes. Irrigation must cover the entire plant for it to be effective, and there must be sufficient water pressure to maintain a balance between freezing and melting ice.

▲ **An overhead canopy will provide several degrees of frost protection for sensitive palms.**

Seed Germination

Germinating a palm seed and growing it into a mature specimen is a rewarding experience. For most palm species germination is relatively easy if you follow some simple guidelines.

■ **Harvesting the fruit** If you're picking fruit from a palm with the aim of germinating the seeds, make certain the fruit is ripe. The fruit of most species changes color from green to red, black, purple, white, or brown when it is ripe. Some fruits on a fruiting stem turn color sooner than others. Pick only the ripe ones and wait for the others to color fully before harvesting them.

■ **Cleaning the seeds** After harvest clean the fruit from the seeds quickly. Place the fruits in a bucket, cover them with room temperature water, and let them soak overnight. Soaking softens the fruit so that you can remove it from the seeds by rubbing it between your hands under the water or by peeling it away from the seed with a knife. Some seeds are surrounded by a matted fiber, but removing the fiber is not necessary. Do not allow the fruit to sit in water too long because it can begin to ferment, killing the embryo.

Caution: Some fruits contain oxalic acid crystals, which can cause severe itching and skin discomfort. Palms that are most toxic are sugar palms (*Arenga*) and fishtail palms (*Caryota*). To a lesser extent macarthur, maya, royal, and spindle palms can also cause irritation. Wear rubber gloves and protective clothing when handling these seeds. Orania palm is the only palm with poisonous seeds if ingested. Handle its seeds with great care.

■ **Washing the seeds** Place the clean seeds in a container filled with water. Soaking serves three functions. The water washes off fungicides that may have been applied to purchased seeds and that can inhibit germination. Immersion also rehydrates the embryo and the endosperm (stored food in the seed), which may have dried out in storage. In addition soaking identifies seeds that tend to be infertile and should

▶ **Allow palm fruits to ripen on the tree if you plan to harvest them for starting new plants. The fruits of sunshine palm turn deep red when they are mature.**

▲ Soak harvested fruits overnight to make removal of the outer fleshy fruit easier. Avoid soaking the seeds so long that they begin to ferment.

▶ **Healthy palm seeds have white endosperm (the food used by the embryo during germination).**

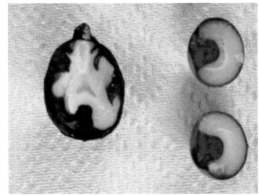

▲ Plant palm seeds at the soil surface. Just barely cover the seeds of small-seeded species, and leave part of the seed exposed for types with large seeds.

be discarded; those are seeds that float after being in the water for 24 to 48 hours.

■ **Selecting a container** After soaking the seeds choose one or more containers in which to plant them. Most palm species germinate well in pots approximately 6 inches deep. Exceptions are bismarck, gingerbread, and ronier palm, all of which send a seedling root down 12 to 18 inches; a deep nursery pot is an ideal germination container for them.

■ **Choosing a soil mix** Use a palm potting mix or one that contains equal parts of peat moss and coarse perlite. Such a mix provides excellent drainage and keeps sufficient moisture around the seed for good germination.

■ **Planting the seeds** Partially fill the germination container with soil, keeping in mind the size of the seed. Place the seed on its side on top of the soil. Add more soil around the seed until it is barely covered—or in the case of a large seed leave the upper one-quarter of the seed exposed.

▲ **Because palm seedlings rapidly develop an extensive root system, use only deep pots for starting seeds.**

▲ **If you plant multiple seeds in one container transplant them to individual pots shortly after they sprout.**

Avoid compressing or packing the soil. Keep the soil loose so it drains well and roots can develop easily. Water the container thoroughly.

You can place multiple seeds in the same container. To help prevent the spread of fungal diseases, space the seeds far enough apart so that they do not touch one another.

■ **Providing warmth** Palm seeds germinate best in warm temperatures. Maintain 90° to 100°F during the day, and 75° to 80°F at night. Keep the germination container in a bright place out of direct sunlight. Water the container thoroughly when the top of the soil becomes dry to the touch.

Palm seeds are slow to germinate. Some species sprout in as little as two to four weeks. Others take 30 to 90 days, and some can take a year or longer. Some species germinate all at once while others germinate sporadically over a year or two. You'll definitely need patience.

■ **Handling seedlings** After a seed has sprouted, the seedling feeds on the endosperm until the first or second true leaf forms. Apply no fertilizer until the second leaf appears. Wait until the first leaf has fully formed to separate seedlings growing in a community pot. Take care not to harm the roots during transplanting. Plant the seedlings in similar soil at the same depth they grew in the germination container. Keep the base of the first leaf even with the top of the soil. Fertilize lightly with a continuous-release or liquid-feed fertilizer. See pages 32 and 35 for more details on feeding.

◄ **Start palm seedlings in a well-drained soil mix such as Miracle-Gro® Cactus, Palm & Citrus Soil.**

PALM PROBLEM SOLVER

Palms establish quickly, are easy to care for, and have few pest and disease problems. Healthy palms resist insect pests and diseases, but occasionally they can be affected by one troublemaker or another. Carefully observe your palms to catch problems before they become severe and difficult to treat. Look for shoots that have died back or leaves that are spotted, discolored, or frizzled. These symptoms indicate that something is wrong with your palm. This chapter will help you diagnose and correct the most common ailments that can strike palms. You'll find descriptions of the various problems along with symptoms to look for and solutions to carry out. (Note that discolored or frizzled leaves may be caused by a nutrient deficiency rather than an insect or disease; see page 35 for remedies.)

Insect pests are more of a nuisance than a severe problem on palms. Most cause little harm to a palm, and the palm usually outgrows any damage. A major exception is the palmetto weevil, which attacks palms from within and is generally not noticed until it is too late. Most insects attack palms that are environmentally stressed, so prevent an assault by providing proper sun exposure, and adequate moisture and fertilizer to keep your palms healthy.

Various fungi cause the most common diseases of palm. Ganoderma butt rot and fusarium wilt can be serious problems, and fungi causing other diseases often move in when a plant is stressed. Relieving the stress on the plant is the long-term solution to preventing the fungus from returning. Lethal yellowing is a serious disease that affects certain popular species of palms. Currently in the United States only South Florida is affected by lethal yellowing. However, a closely related disease affects date palms in Central Florida and South Texas.

▼ **Hurricane-force winds and periodic deluges are environmental stresses that some palms may have to withstand.**

INSECT PESTS

◁ **Palm leaf skeletonizer damage shows up on the leaf surface.**

▽ **Palm aphids are sucking insects that are most likely to attack tender new growth.**

Palm aphid

A sucking insect that can infest a palm in large numbers, palm aphid appears mainly on the newest growth. It looks similar to soft brown scale except that it is surrounded by a ring of white wax. Like mealybugs, palm aphid excretes honeydew, which sooty mold fungus feeds on. The honeydew attracts ants which farm the aphids to develop large colonies of the pest. Treat palm aphid with insecticidal soap or horticultural oil. Insecticides containing dimethoate or acephate are also effective.

Palm leaf skeletonizer

Palm leaf skeletonizer is a small caterpillar that feeds in large numbers on both surfaces of palm leaves. It produces a great deal of fibrous excrement, called frass, that is the primary sign of infestation. An insecticide containing carbaryl (Sevin) or the biological insecticide, *Bacillus thuringiensis kurstaki* (Btk), is somewhat effective in controlling this pest.

Mealybugs

Numerous species of mealybugs affect palms. Some of these sucking insects feed on the roots and can't be seen unless the soil is disturbed. But most infestations occur in the palm bud, where new leaves emerge. The insects create large colonies and secrete honeydew, a sticky material, that sooty mold fungus feeds on. Treat mealybugs with insecticidal soap, horticultural oil, or insecticides containing acephate or dimethoate. Ants do not feed on palms, but they farm mealybugs for the honeydew they excrete. They promote large colonies of the mealybugs and thus indirectly harm palms. Controlling the ant population with insecticides will reduce the number of mealybugs.

▷ **Palmetto weevil is a beetle with a long snout. Its larvae tunnel into the heart of the palm, eventually killing the tree.**

▽ **Mealybugs can attack palms or cycads. They appear as cottony white masses on leaves and stems.**

Palmetto weevil

Palmetto weevil is a large beetle that is attracted to stressed palms. Cabbage, Canary Island date, and other large palms are its primary targets. The adult weevil lays eggs in the leaf bases. The eggs hatch into large larvae that tunnel into the palm heart, where they feed. In time this pest destroys the heart, killing the palm. You may not notice symptoms until the leaf crown topples over. Minimizing transplant stress in newly planted palms will reduce the chance of attack by palmetto weevil. Pheromone traps have been useful in Central and South America in reducing weevil infestation, but currently the traps are not widely available in the United States. Remove and destroy affected trees before adults emerge to halt the spread of the pest.

Saddleback caterpillar

Feeding on the underside of palm leaves, saddleback caterpillar chews large holes in the foliage. It has poisonous spines that can cause a burning sensation like a bee sting when they come in contact with bare skin. The biological insecticide Btk is effective in controlling young caterpillars.

Scale insects

Magnolia white scale, cottony cushion scale, Florida red scale, thread scale, and soft brown scale are among the most common scale insects that affect palms. These sucking insects, which are visible to the naked eye, tend to feed on new growth. Horticultural oil is an effective control, but repeated sprayings are necessary. The first

△ **The saddleback caterpillar chews the foliage of palms creating holes in the leaves.**

◁ **Soft brown scale is one of several scale insects that can attack palms.**

treatment kills active crawlers (immature scale insects that have not developed a shell) and adults, but eggs and young scale insects under the shells of adults can survive. Spray the plant again a week to 10 days later to control the newly hatched crawlers and young scale insects that were protected under the shells of adults. Insecticides containing dimethoate or acephate are also effective, but also require repeat treatment for good control.

△ **Spider mites cause stippling on palm leaves and may form webbing as well.**

Spider mites

These pests—they're not true insects but instead members of the spider family—are common on palms grown indoors or in dry conditions. Although many species of spider mites feed on palm leaves, the most notorious is the two-spotted mite. *Chamaedorea* species are particularly prone to spider mites. Symptoms include yellow spotting or stippling in the leaf. In severe infestations the leaf becomes pale or appears washed out and webbing is evident on the underside. The mites are small, appearing as tiny, moving dots. A hand lens is helpful in seeing them. Forceful sprays of water, insecticidal soap, and horticultural oil are effective in controlling mites, as are miticides. A predator mite, *Phytoseiulus persimilis*, is used as a mite control in some greenhouses, but it is ineffective outdoors.

DISEASES

Lethal yellowing

A deadly disease caused by a phytoplasma (a bacterium without cell walls), lethal yellowing is commonly spread by the planthopper *Myndus crudus*, a sucking insect that feeds on palm plant tissue. After feeding on an infected palm, the planthopper moves to a healthy one and transmits the disease when it begins to feed. Controlling the insect is difficult because it is extremely mobile and widespread in warm, humid areas such as South Florida.

■ **Symptoms** Some palms are unaffected by lethal yellowing and others are highly susceptible. (See the list of susceptible palms below right.) The initial symptoms include blackening of flower and fruit stems and premature fruit drop. In most species the leaves turn yellow, grey, or brown starting with the oldest and gradually moving into the new leaves. Finally the newest leaf spear dies and the entire crown falls off. In some species the newest leaf spear dies before other leaves discolor.

■ **Treatment** There is no cure for lethal yellowing, but periodic injections of the antibiotic oxytetracycline hydrochloride (OTC) prevents the disease from progressing. A source for this treatment is Tree Saver®, a company that specializes in lethal yellowing treatment programs. For a more detailed description of the treatment see the company's website palmtreesaver.com. Once treatment is started, it should continue for the life of the palm. If treatment stops symptoms may reappear and the palm may die. No strains of coconut are known to be resistant.

▶ **Yellowing of the oldest leaves is a normal occurence in palms. Don't confuse it with lethal yellowing in which the yellowing progresses to younger leaves.**

◀ **Lethal yellowing eventually causes all leaves to turn brown and die, leading to the death of the tree.**

▶ **The antibiotic OTC prevents lethal yellowing from following its usual course in palms regularly injected with the chemical.**

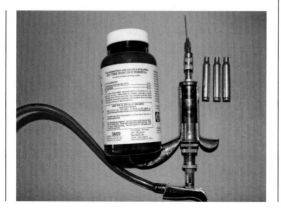

Fusarium wilt

Fusarium oxysporum canariensis affects Canary Island date palm and to a much lesser degree date, Senegal date, and silver date palms. The disease has been in California since the 1970s and in Florida since 1994. On infected palms the leaflets on only one side of the leaf stem of the oldest leaves turn brown. A reddish or dark brown stripe along the leaf stem develops. The oldest leaves eventually turn completely brown. The symptoms move to the next oldest leaves until finally the newest leaf spear is left to die. The process can take a few months to two years. There is no treatment for fusarium wilt, but its spread can be halted by disinfecting pruning tools between trees.

PALM SPECIES SUSCEPTIBLE TO LETHAL YELLOWING

Arikury palm	Formosa palm
Cabada palm	Kentia palm
Canary Island date palm	*Manila palm
	Mazari palm
Chinese fan palm	Princess palm
Clumping fishtail palm	Seashore palm
*Coconut palm	Senegal date palm
Curly kentia palm	Silver date palm
Date palm	Spindle palm
Dwarf majesty palm	Sunshine palm
*Dwarf pritchardia	*Thurston palm
*Fiji fan palm	Triangle palm
Footstool palm	Windmill palm

* extremely susceptible

Ganoderma butt rot

No palm species is immune to the lethal disease ganoderma butt rot. A palm that contracts ganoderma shows few outward symptoms until the palm is nearly dead. The fungus affects the lower 4 to 5 feet of the trunk (the butt of the tree), rotting the woody tissue from the inside out. Eventually the leaves wilt and turn brown except for the center spear leaf. Just before the palm dies or shortly thereafter, a distinctive conk (shelflike fungal growth) appears on the outside of the trunk near the base of the tree. A mature conk releases millions of spores that can spread by wind or water. To keep the spores from dispersing remove conks when they appear, wrap them in plastic, and dispose of them. Remove and dispose of the entire palm to prevent infection of other palms. Ganoderma survives in the soil, so avoid planting other palms in the same location. No known cure exists for ganoderma butt rot.

Other fungal diseases

■ **Leaf spot fungi** A number of leaf spot fungi cause yellow or dark brown spotting of leaflets. These include helminthosporium, anthracnose, false smut, and *Pestalotiopsis*. The fungi more commonly attack young palms than older ones, and the attacks often occur on palms that are under stress from overwatering or poor drainage in mucky soils. Correct the predisposing stress factor to solve the problem. Your local nursery professional also may suggest a fungicide application.

▲ **Ganoderma butt rot affects the lower portion of the trunk first. A spongy white growth will develop on the outside of the trunk.**

▲ **As the ganoderma conk matures it turns brown. Remove the conk to prevent spores from spreading to other trees.**

■ **Phytophthora bud rot** This soilborne disease can be a problem during hot, wet summers. The new leaf spear becomes discolored and wilts, followed by discoloration of the next newest leaves. In early stages of the disease a bud drench with a fungicide containing fosetyl-Al, mefenoxam, or propamocarb can be effective. If the new spear leaf pulls out easily and the next newest leaves are already brown, it may be too late for treatment to be helpful.

■ **Sooty mold** This fungus often feeds on honeydew produced by mealybug, palm aphid, and scale insect infestations, forming a black covering on the leaves. Sooty mold does not attack the plant directly and easily washes off. To prevent the problem from reoccurring, control the sucking insects that produce honeydew.

▲ **Helminthosporium leaf spot causes yellow spots that may develop brown centers on palm foliage.**

▲ **Sooty mold appears as a powdery black coating on the leaf. Control sucking insects that produce honeydew to manage the fungus.**

▲ **Phytophthora bud rot spreads through the soil or air. The spear leaf is first to die, and older leaves may remain green for months afterward.**

CULTURAL AND ENVIRONMENTAL PROBLEMS

Improper placement

A palm may outgrow the area in which it is located, a situation that often happens to palms planted in screen enclosures, under overhangs, or close to buildings. Palms cannot be trimmed like other plants to fit a certain area. They will not regenerate from the trunk and if their leaves are removed they will begin to decline. Cutting the leaves back also makes a palm less ornamental. Think carefully before you decide on a planting location, and choose a palm that will not outgrow the allotted space.

WIND-RESISTANT PALMS

Blue latan palm
Bottle palm
Cabbage palm
Pindo palm
Princess palm
Silver thatch palm
Solitaire palm
Spindle palm
Sunshine palm
Thatch palm

Lightning

In areas with frequent thunderstorms it is common to see palms, especially tall ones, that have been hit by lightning. Symptoms of lightning damage are immediate wilting of most leaves and various types of damage to the trunk: oozing sap from small cracks all the way up and down large cracks, and burn or scorch marks. If most or all the leaves on a palm tree wilt overnight and hang limp next to the trunk, a lightning strike is the most likely cause. Depending on the severity of the strike, the palm may recover over time or gradually die. No specific treatment speeds recovery; continue normal watering and feeding.

▲ Lightning can cause scorch marks or cracks to develop on the trunk or induce sudden wilting of the leaves.

▲ These triangle palms were planted too close to this building. They are now misshapen because fronds on the side of the building had to be removed to prevent damage to the wall and siding.

Hurricanes

A hurricane can devastate a landscape but palms are able to withstand hurricane-force winds better than other woody plants. They bend in the wind without breaking and their leaves remain attached. Some palms fare much better than others. Those native to hurricane-prone areas hold up better than those from rain forest or mountainous habitats. If you are concerned about wind damage to your palms, plant wind-resistant palms. Some of the best for this purpose are listed above.

▲ Although palm trunks are quite pliable, excessive winds associated with hurricanes can cause them to snap.

Power line decline

When tall palms are planted under or near power lines a phenomenon called power line decline can occur. Leaves that touch the line turn yellow or brown from electromagnetic fields. On a tree planted directly below the power line, many of the leaves turn yellow or brown, apparently due to the electromagnetic field generated by the power line. Leaves up to 5 feet away can turn yellow and die, and prolonged exposure may kill the whole palm. Avoid planting palms near power lines. If your palm suffers from power line decline, consider calling in a professional to move it—transplanting a palm growing near power lines is extremely dangerous.

Salt spray

Palms that grow close to the coast are exposed to salt spray in the air. Prevailing winds can carry the salt spray a significant distance from the shore. Palms that naturally grow in habitats close to salt water tend to be much more salt-tolerant than rain forest or inland palms. Using palms that don't tolerate salt in a coastal landscape can lead to severe leaf burn and death of the palms. Consult the list at right for salt-tolerant palms that do well in coastal gardens.

▶ Electromagnetic fields generated by a power line can cause dieback on a palm growing near the line.

SALT-TOLERANT PALMS

Buccaneer palm
Cabbage palm
Coconut palm
Date palm
Princess palm
Saw palmetto
Seashore palm
Silver thatch palm
Sunshine palm
Thatch palm

Unadapted palms

It's natural for gardeners to try to extend the growing range of plants they like, but trying to grow palms unsuited to your climate can be frustrating. Palms that thrive in cool, mountainous habitats will not do well in the hot lowlands of Florida. Likewise palms that flourish in the wet Amazon basin will not succeed in the dry hills of Southern California. Your pH— the acidity or alkalinity of your soil— also affects how well different palms adapt to your garden. If you have a palm that is not doing well despite proper care, research its native habitat to find out if it is unsuited to your climate or consult a knowledgeable grower or specialist at a palm nursery to find out what conditions your palm needs.

◀ Salt spray damage shows up as browning on foliage. Often the windward side of the tree is most severely affected.

GALLERY OF PALMS

▼ Palms in the landscape evoke a feeling of the tropics. With a diversity of heights, shapes, and environmental adaptations, they can form the backbone of the landscape or provide a stately accent. From fan-shape fronds with silvery blue coloration to feathery deep green fronds, you'll be able to find palms that fit your color preference. Some tower over the landscape, creating a magnificent silhouette against the sky; other low-growers make an effective screen or groundcover.

On the following pages you will find descriptions, care information, and suggested uses for more than 175 species of palms, including the ones most widely grown. A few are rare, but they have unusual characteristics and are included to show the diversity of this incredible family of plants.

The palms are alphabetized by botanical name, with a pronunciation guide to help you say it properly. The common name is also listed, but be aware that these names are unreliable; one plant may be known by various common names in different regions, and some species share the same common name. The botanical names are standard and unique throughout the world.

In each description a bulleted list highlights the key attributes of the palm. **Size** The height and width given is for a mature palm. A range is provided because the ultimate size depends on growing conditions and region.

Light This refers to the amount of sunlight that the palm prefers.

■ **Heavy shade** means little or no direct sunlight during the day.

■ **Moderate shade** means no direct sunlight for at least half the day with filtered sunlight at other times.

■ **Light shade** refers to an area with lightly filtered sunlight.

■ **Full sun** means no shade throughout most of the day; at least 6 to 8 hours of direct sun.

Water This refers to the amount of water that the palm needs.

■ **Drought tolerant** indicates that you should water only in a severe drought.

■ **Low** means water during dry spells.

■ **Moderate** tells you to water once a week.

■ **Wet** means water the root zone three to four times per week.

■ **Aquatic** indicates the soil should always be saturated.

Minimum temperature This is the lowest temperature at which the palm will survive, although it may suffer minor damage. The temperature is based on a short cold snap lasting two to six hours; prolonged cold can be far more detrimental to palms than a brief dip in temperature.

Features This section briefly describes the palm type and key ornamental features.

Acoelorraphe wrightii
ay-see-lo-RAY-fee REYE-tee-eye
Paurotis palm, Everglades palm

- **Size:** 12–20'H×12–20'W
- **Light:** Light shade to full sun
- **Water:** Drought tolerant
- **Minimum temperature:** 25°F
- **Features:** Multitrunk fan palm with small teeth on leaf stems

Paurotis palm

A native of Florida, the West Indies, and eastern Central America, paurotis palm forms a large clump of trunks that are 2 to 4 inches thick and are covered in old brown leaf bases. The semicircular leaves are bright green on top with a slight silver tone underneath, and the leaf stems are armed with short teeth. Small shiny black fruit develops.
Care: A slow to moderate grower, paurotis palm does best in humusy neutral to acidic soil that stays wet. The plant is drought-tolerant and has slight salt tolerance. It occasionally shows a potassium deficiency, which can be solved with regular feeding with slow-release potassium.
Recommended uses: Paurotis palm makes a handsome large specimen; for an airy look, cut out the smaller trunks and leave only the taller ones. Paurotis is also an effective screen; use several of them alone or in combination with other plants to create an impenetrable wall of foliage.

Acrocomia aculeata
ak-ro-KO-mee-uh uh-kyoo-lee-AHT-uh
Gru-gru palm, macaw palm

- **Size:** 25–40'H×15–20'W
- **Light:** Full sun
- **Water:** Drought tolerant
- **Minimum temperature:** 25–30°F
- **Features:** Single-trunk feather-leaf palm covered in sharp spines

Gru-gru palm is a highly variable palm that was once considered to be several different species because plants of different origins (it is native to Mexico, Central and South America, and the Antilles) have different appearances. The trunk, growing to 18 inches thick, is covered in 1- to 3-inch needlelike spines. The spiny leaves vary from bright green to grayish green. The leaflets radiate out in all directions, giving the leaf a feathery appearance. The fruit is yellowish green to brown.
Care: The form once classified as *A. totai* is much more cold-tolerant than the other forms, leading to the range in minimum temperature cited above. Gru-gru palm grows moderately fast and prefers well-drained acidic or neutral soil. With proper feeding the plant tolerates slightly alkaline soil. It has excellent drought tolerance and no salt tolerance.
Recommended uses: Although gru-gru palm can be striking on its own, it looks better when grouped or surrounded by other plantings.

Gru-gru palm

Acrocomia crispa
ak-ro-KO-mee-uh KRISP-uh
Cuban belly palm

- **Size:** 40–45'H×12–15'W
- **Light:** Full sun
- **Water:** Drought tolerant
- **Minimum temperature:** 30°F
- **Features:** Single-trunk feather-leaf palm covered in sharp spines

Cuban belly palm

Formerly known as *Gastrococos crispa*, this native of Cuba has a gray trunk covered in needlelike black spines. The trunk develops a large rounded bulge that looks like a protruding belly and adds to the charm of the plant. The 8- to 10-foot-long medium to dark green leaves are spiny. The fruit is yellowish orange.
Care: Cuban belly palm does well in any soil that drains easily. It appreciates regular water and fertilizer. The plant withstands short dry spells and has some salt tolerance. It grows slowly when young, and then puts on a rapid growth spurt during which the belly forms; afterward it grows at a moderate rate.
Recommended uses: Cuban belly palm looks best planted in an open space where its handsome form can be fully appreciated. A staggered grouping with a low groundcover underneath is a splendid sight.

Adonidia merrillii
ad-o-NID-ee-uh mer-RIL-ee-eye

Manila palm, Christmas palm

- **Size: 15–25'H×10–12'W**
- **Light: Moderate shade to full sun**
- **Water: Drought tolerant**
- **Minimum temperature: 30°F**
- **Features: Single-trunk feather-leaf palm with crownshaft**

Manila palm

This palm hails from the Philippines but is a common fixture in landscapes throughout the world. The gray trunk is about 5 to 8 inches in diameter. The crownshaft is light green, and the 4- to 6-foot-long leaves light to medium green. The fact that the fruit turns crimson at Christmastime is responsible for one of the palm's common names.
Care: Even though still widely cultivated in South Florida, the Manila palm is highly susceptible to lethal yellowing disease. It grows well in well-drained acidic or alkaline soil and tolerates some salt and short periods of drought.
Recommended uses: Manila palm is ideally suited to smaller yards as a specimen (it needs no other plants around it to be noticed) or in small groupings. It is equally at home in a formal or wild tropical garden. The palm also does well in a well-lit indoor setting such as an atrium.

Aiphanes aculeata
ay-EE-fa-neez uh-kyoo-lee-AHT-uh

Ruffle palm

- **Size: 20–30'H×8–12'W**
- **Light: Moderate to light shade**
- **Water: Moderate**
- **Minimum temperature: 32°F**
- **Features: Single-trunk feather-leaf palm covered in sharp spines**

Black needlelike spines cover the trunk and leaves of this palm native to northern South America. The trunk grows to 6 inches in diameter. The 4- to 6-foot-long bright green leaves are arranged in groups along the leaf stem with the leaflets radiating in all directions. The fruit is bright orange to red.
Care: Ruffle palm has no unusual nutrient requirements, and it flourishes in well-drained acidic or alkaline soil that contains some organic matter. It tolerates salt only slightly. The plant is a moderate grower that does not tolerate drying out. It will adapt to light shade or full sun when older.
Recommended uses: This unusual and ornamental palm looks best in a grouping under the canopy of a tall tree. It needs contrasting foliage underneath and behind it to show off really well. The sharp, brittle spines make this one plant you'd be wise to admire from a slight distance—keep it away from walkways and other high-traffic areas, and take care when handling the plant.

Ruffle palm; ripe fruit (inset)

Allagoptera arenaria
al-uh-GAHP-ter-uh ar-eh-NAR-ee-uh

Seashore palm

- **Size: 6–10'H×8–15'W**
- **Light: Full sun**
- **Water: Drought tolerant**
- **Minimum temperature: 25°F**
- **Features: Single-trunk branching feather-leaf palm with subterranean trunk**

Seashore palm

This native of Brazilian coastal dunes usually makes a short cluster of very feathery leaves from 4 to 6 feet long. Its subterranean trunk occasionally emerges above ground. The narrow leaflets are deep dark green on top and silvery underneath. The fruit is unusual because it is densely packed in a pineapple shape and even smells like a pineapple when it ripens.
Care: When grown in well-drained sandy soil, seashore palm is extremely easy to care for. It grows slowly, then picks up speed as it matures. The plant does fine in light shade but looks best in full sun. It may be the most salt-tolerant of all palms. Seashore palm rarely shows any disease or nutrient problems other than being slightly susceptible to lethal yellowing.
Recommended uses: Use this beautiful shrubby palm by itself or in masses as a low screen. It is one of the best palms for a seaside landscape, and it also does well in containers outdoors.

Allagoptera caudescens
al-uh-GAHP-ter-uh kaw-DES-enz
Buri palm

- **Size: 25–30'H×10–12'W**
- **Light: Light shade to full sun**
- **Water: Low to moderate**
- **Minimum temperature: 30°F**
- **Features: Single-trunk feather-leaf palm with silver leaf undersides**

Buri palm

Formerly named *Polyandrococos caudescens*, this beautiful Brazilian native has a grayish trunk about 8 inches thick that is often covered in old leaf bases. The leaves, growing to 10 feet long and made up of leaflets gathered in groups along the leaf stem, are gray-green on top and silver underneath. The new, nearly vertical leaves, which put their silver undersides on view, make a showy contrast with the older, more lax leaves, which display their gray-green upper surfaces. The greenish brown fruit is borne on a spiky, pendulous bract.
Care: Buri palm does well in acidic or alkaline soil. It prefers regular water and rarely shows nutrient deficiencies. The plant has a slight salt tolerance. Its growth rate varies from slow to moderately fast. The plant prefers light shade particularly when young.
Recommended uses: Buri palm is handsome as a single palm under a high-canopy tree with a low groundcover beneath. It is even more attractive when several are planted in a grouping.

Archontophoenix alexandrae
ar-kont-o-FEE-nix al-ek-ZAN-dray-ee
King palm

- **Size: 35–50'H×15–18'W**
- **Light: Full sun**
- **Water: Low to moderate**
- **Minimum temperature: 30°F**
- **Features: Single-trunk feather-leaf palm with crownshaft**

King palm comes from Queensland, Australia, where it can grow to 80 feet tall. The thick gray to brown trunk grows to 1 foot thick. The crownshaft is olive green, and the 6- to 10-foot leaves are bright green on top and slightly silver underneath. The fruit is crimson.
Care: This palm requires acidic soil, regular water, and a sunny location to do well. It does not tolerate alkaline soil and has only a slight tolerance for salt. The plant grows moderately fast in the right conditions.
Recommended uses: King palm is aptly named for its majestic presence in any landscape large enough to accommodate its stately size. It works well as a stand-alone palm but looks even grander in a grouping. Although it doesn't need companion plants, it is attractive underplanted with a low groundcover.

King palm

Archontophoenix cunninghamiana
ar-kont-o-FEE-nix kun-ing-ham-ee-AYN-uh
Piccabeen palm, Bungalow palm

- **Size: 30–45'H×10–15'W**
- **Light: Light shade to full sun**
- **Water: Low to moderate**
- **Minimum temperature: 28°F**
- **Features: Single-trunk feather-leaf palm with crownshaft**

Piccabeen palm

A similar but somewhat smaller version of king palm, this Australian native has an 8- to 10-inch-diameter trunk. It, too, has an olive green crownshaft and bright green leaves 6 to 10 feet long. However, its leaves lack the silvery undersides characteristic of king palm. The fruit branches are longer, with crimson fruit.
Care: Piccabeen palm prefers acidic soil and regular water. It tolerates little salt. Its growth rate is slightly slower than that of king palm. The plant shows some heat stress in South Florida, where it prefers light shade. Elsewhere it does better in full sun. This plant is the cold-hardiest of all crownshaft palms.
Recommended uses: Piccabeen is a regal palm that looks best when several are planted together, although it also stands out as a single palm on its own or with a low groundcover underneath it.

Archontophoenix purpurea
ar-kont-o-FEE-nix pur-PUR-ee-uh

Purple king palm

- **Size:** 30–45'H×12–20'W
- **Light:** Light shade to full sun
- **Water:** Moderate
- **Minimum temperature:** 28°F
- **Features:** Single-trunk feather-leaf palm with purple crownshaft

Purple king palm

This palm comes from Mount Lewis in Queensland, Australia. It looks like king palm except that it has an eyecatching purple crownshaft. Otherwise its description is the same as for king palm, although its trunk can be up to 18 inches in diameter.
Care: Like both king and piccabeen palms, this plant needs acidic soil and regular water to thrive. The plant does not tolerate salt. It is a bit slower growing than the other two palms. Coming from a 4,000-foot elevation, it finds the hot summer nights in Florida difficult and grows better in Southern California or Hawaii.
Recommended uses: Because of its purple crownshaft and somewhat bulkier stature, purple king palm works well as a specimen and is superb in a grouping. It needs no other plantings underneath, although a low groundcover makes an attractive accent.

Areca catechu
uh-REEK-uh KAT-eh-koo

Betel nut palm

- **Size:** 35–50'H×10–12'W
- **Light:** Light shade to full sun
- **Water:** Moderate to wet
- **Minimum temperature:** 32°F
- **Features:** Single-trunk feather-leaf palm with crownshaft

The betel nut palm's exact origin is unknown but believed to be somewhere in Southeast Asia. The leaves, crownshaft, and upper part of the trunk are bright dark green. Contrasting white rings, where the old leaves fall off, embellish the 6-inch-thick trunk. The stiffly arched leaves can reach 6 feet long. The yellow to crimson fruit is quite showy when ripe. The seeds, which are sold in native markets, produce a mild narcotic effect when chewed with lime and pepper leaves.
Care: Fast-growing betel nut palm prefers acidic wet soil that is humusy and drains well. It does not tolerate being completely dried out. The plant has no special fertilizer demands and little salt tolerance.
Recommended uses: A staggered grouping of betel nut palms is a sight to behold. The visual effect is often lost when the palm is used as a specimen plant. A young plant looks best in light shade, but as it matures it becomes quite at home in full sun.

Betel nut palm

Areca triandra
uh-REEK-uh try-AN-druh

Three anther palm

- **Size:** 15–25'H×12–20'W
- **Light:** Moderate to light shade
- **Water:** Moderate
- **Minimum temperature:** 32°F
- **Features:** Multitrunk feather-leaf palm with crownshaft

Three anther palm

This native of the Philippines and other parts of Southeast Asia occasionally has a single trunk, but more commonly multiple trunks. The trunks are usually no more than 3 inches in diameter, and the leaves are about 4 to 6 feet long and not as stiff as those of betel nut palm. The crownshaft, leaves, and upper trunk are bright dark green while the lower trunk is grayish. The fruit is generally crimson. The overall visual effect is quite ornamental.
Care: Three anther palm comes from wet, acidic sites but will tolerate neutral or slightly alkaline soil that is humusy and drains well. Grow it in light to moderate shade. This moderate grower does well with regular water and fertilizer. It has no tolerance for drying out completely and little tolerance for salt.
Recommended uses: This palm stands out beautifully when planted behind or on either side of broadleaf plants that contrast in texture and form.

Areca vestiaria
uh-REEK-uh ves-tee-AIR-ee-uh

Orange collar palm

- **Size:** 12–20'H×8–12'W
- **Light:** Moderate shade
- **Water:** Moderate
- **Minimum temperature:** 32°F
- **Features:** Single- or multitrunk palm with orange crownshaft

Orange collar palm

The crownshaft of the aptly named orange collar palm, a native of Indonesia, is its most striking feature. The color ranges from light orange to nearly bright red. The trunks are 3 to 4 inches in diameter and sit atop a mass of short stilt roots (aboveground brace roots). The 5- to 6-foot-long leaves are bright green. The fruit is yellow to orangish red.

Care: This palm prefers acidic or neutral soil that contains some organic matter and is well drained. It does not tolerate drought or salt. A moderate grower, the plant has no special nutrient needs. It can tolerate slightly more cold than other species in the genus.

Recommended uses: Because orange collar palm is a standout, plant it in a spot where you can truly appreciate its beauty. Anyone walking through a landscape and chancing upon this palm will find it a visual sensation.

Arenga engleri
uh-RENG-uh ENG-ler-eye

Formosa palm, dwarf sugar palm

- **Size:** 8–12'H×10–15'W
- **Light:** Light shade to full sun
- **Water:** Drought tolerant to low
- **Minimum temperature:** 25°F
- **Features:** Multitrunk feather-leaf palm with black fibers

Native to the Ryukyu Islands of Japan, this attractive palm has leaves that are dark green on top and light silver underneath. The trunk is covered in black fibers, which accentuates the foliage even more. Take care in handling the yellow to orange fruit, which contains oxalic acid crystals, a strong skin irritant. Like other species of *Arenga,* Formosa palm is monocarpic, meaning that once a trunk has finished fruiting it dies. Additional trunks sprout, keeping the palm very full.

Care: Moderately fast-growing Formosa palm thrives in acidic to slightly alkaline wet soil that is well drained. Its salt tolerance is low. Other than having a slight susceptibility to lethal yellowing disease, it does not require special care other than regular feeding. In light shade the leaves stretch, giving the plant an even more feathery look.

Recommended uses: A group of Formosa palms creates an excellent screen, and a single palm on its own makes an attractive specimen plant.

Formosa palm

Arenga hookeriana
uh-RENG-uh hook-air-ee-AHN-uh

Hooker's fishtail palm

- **Size:** 3–5'H×3–5'W
- **Light:** Heavy to moderate shade
- **Water:** Moderate
- **Minimum temperature:** 32°F
- **Features:** Multitrunk feather-leaf palm with undivided leaves

Hooker's fishtail palm

This small palm native to Thailand and Malaysia has thin trunks less than an inch thick. The leaves, which are medium green on top and silvery underneath, are 1 to 2 feet long and quite variable. The most sought-after form has undivided, diamond-shape leaves that are deeply lobed. The plant produces small red fruit. Like Formosa palm and other species of *Arenga,* this palm is monocarpic—a trunk dies after fruiting, but new trunks continue to sprout.

Care: The plant, which grows at a moderate rate, thrives in acidic soil that is humusy and well drained. It appreciates high humidity and does not tolerate dry conditions or salt.

Recommended uses: With its unique leaves and small stature, this palm is well suited as an accent in a rain forest setting or next to a patio. Place it where it can be viewed up close, and partner it with short groundcover plants that will not detract from its beauty.

Arenga pinnata
uh-RENG-uh pin-NAY-tuh
Black sugar palm

- **Size: 40–60'H×25–35'W**
- **Light: Full sun**
- **Water: Drought tolerant to low**
- **Minimum temperature: 28°F**
- **Features: Single-trunk feather-leaf palm with black fibers**

Black sugar palm

Black sugar palm is well named for the persistent black fibers covering the 2-foot-diameter trunk. The leaves, which can reach 30 feet long, are deep dark green on top and silver underneath. Like most species in the genus, this palm begins flowering at the top of the trunk, with flowers gradually emerging from old leaf bases down to the ground over about a three-year span. Once the palm has finished fruiting, it dies.

Black sugar palm has been heavily cultivated for so long that its native origin is unclear, but it may be from Indonesia. The trunk sap is turned into sugary treats as well as an alcoholic beverage.
Care: This palm grows equally well in acidic to somewhat alkaline soil. As long as it has enough moisture and regular fertilizer, it grows rapidly. Its tolerance for salt is low.
Recommended uses: Black sugar palm needs plenty of room to grow. It is an outstanding landscape specimen on its own or with contrasting large palms or other trees.

Arenga tremula
uh-RENG-uh TREM-yoo-luh
Dwarf sugar palm

- **Size: 8–12'H×10–15'W**
- **Light: Light shade to full sun**
- **Water: Drought tolerant**
- **Minimum temperature: 30°F**
- **Features: Multitrunk feather-leaf palm with black fibers**

A native of the Philippines, this plant resembles its relative Formosa palm. The trunks, 3 to 4 inches in diameter, are covered in black fibers. The 6- to 8-foot-long leaves are made up of leaflets that are more widely spaced and narrower than those of Formosa palm, and they may be lighter green but with the same silver cast underneath. On this species the fruit is red, but it also contains skin-irritating oxalic acid crystals.
Care: Dwarf sugar palm prefers a humusy acidic soil but it tolerates slightly alkaline conditions. The plant grows at a moderate rate. It has only a slight tolerance for salt. This palm doesn't require any special nutrients and has few disease problems. It looks best in light shade, though older plants tolerate full sun well.
Recommended uses: Surround dwarf sugar palm with other lush, lower-growing tropical vegetation or let it stand alone as a ferny statement in an expanse of lawn. Plant several for an excellent screen.

Dwarf sugar palm

Asterogyne martiana
ass-ter-AH-ji-nee mar-tee-AHN-uh
Polaris palm

- **Size: 4–6'H×3–4'W**
- **Light: Heavy to moderate shade**
- **Water: Moderate to wet**
- **Minimum temperature: 35°F**
- **Features: Single-trunk feather-leaf palm with undivided leaves**

Polaris palm

The trunk of this Central and northern South American native, usually covered in old brown leaf bases, is just a little over an inch thick. Each 2-foot-long leaf is shaped like a fish's tail. The new growth is sometimes pinkish red while the older leaves are rich green. The small oval fruit is deep red.
Care: Polaris palm requires exacting conditions to do well: well-drained acidic soil with organic matter mixed in, regular water (but not conditions that are either too wet or too droughty), constant high humidity, and regular fertilizer. The plant grows at a moderate rate and has no salt tolerance.
Recommended uses: If you meet this palm's demands, it will become a star in an understory landscape. A grouping of several polaris palms is spectacular.

Astrocaryum mexicanum
ass-tro-KAIR-ee-um mex-ih-KAHN-um
Mexican astrocaryum

- **Size:** 15–20'H×10–12'W
- **Light:** Moderate to light shade
- **Water:** Moderate to wet
- **Minimum temperature:** 32°F
- **Features:** Single-trunk feather-leaf palm with spines

Mexican astrocaryum

Found throughout southern Mexico and Central America, Mexican astrocaryum has flat black spines covering a trunk that is 2 to 3 inches thick. The leaves, which can be 6 feet long or longer, are spiny underneath the midrib. The leaflets vary in width and are dark khaki green on top and silvery green underneath. The spiny fruit is brown.

Care: This palm does best in moderate shade—the leaves grow longer, giving the plant an even more graceful look than when it's located in more light. It can succeed in either acidic or alkaline soil that contains some organic matter and drains well. The plant has no tolerance for salt or for drying out. It has no special fertilizer needs, and it can tolerate an occasional short dip below freezing.

Recommended uses: Mexican astrocaryum belongs in a lush tropical setting. For unsurpassed beauty plant several in a group.

Attalea cohune
at-TAL-ee-uh ko-HOO-nee
Cohune palm

- **Size:** 50–80'H×30–40'W
- **Light:** Full sun
- **Water:** Drought tolerant to low
- **Minimum temperature:** 30°F
- **Features:** Single-trunk feather-leaf palm

Native to Mexico, Belize, and Guatemala, cohune palm has a trunk to 2 feet in diameter or more. In young plants the trunk is usually covered in old leaf bases, but these shed eventually. The dark grassy green leaves, which are held stiffly, can be more than 25 feet long. They twist at their midpoint vertical to the ground. The brown fruit is the size of a small hen's egg.

Care: Cohune palm, which grows at a slow to moderate rate, does best in well-drained alkaline to slightly acidic soil. It has no special fertilizer needs, and it does not tolerate salt or high winds well.

Recommended uses: Cohune palm is a massive tree that requires a large landscape to keep it in proportion. It is magnificent as a specimen plant. And if your landscape can handle more than one, you'll find that the effect of walking beneath their arching fronds is like being in a large cathedral.

Cohune palm

Attalea phalerata
at-TAL-ee-uh fal-eh-RAHT-uh
Cusi palm

- **Size:** 25–35'H×25–30'W
- **Light:** Full sun
- **Water:** Drought tolerant to low
- **Minimum temperature:** 30°F
- **Features:** Single-trunk feather-leaf palm

Cusi palm

A native of Peru, Bolivia, and Brazil, cusi palm has a trunk to 3 feet thick or more that is covered in old leaf bases. The trunk itself is short, but the 20-foot dark green leaves give the plant plenty of height—and width. The leaflets radiate out in all directions, giving the plant a very feathery look. The fruit is brown.

Care: Slow-growing cusi palm succeeds in alkaline to slightly acidic soil that is well drained. The plant appreciates regular water and fertilizer, but tolerates drought. It has little tolerance for salt.

Recommended uses: This stocky but stately palm requires a great deal of space. Use cusi palm as a specimen—or if your yard is big enough, plant a grouping for a formal or tropical ambience.

Bactris gasipaes
BAK-tris GAS-ih-peez

Peach palm

- **Size:** 35–50'H×15–30'W
- **Light:** Light shade to full sun
- **Water:** Moderate to wet
- **Minimum temperature:** 32°F
- **Features:** Multitrunk feather-leaf palm with spines

Peach palm

This palm has been cultivated for so long that its exact origin is unknown, but it is from somewhere in Central or South America. The trunk is typically 6 to 12 inches thick and covered in needlelike spines. The 6- to 10-foot-long, emerald green leaves are also covered in spines. The fruit, which may be yellow to red, is a favored food either fresh or canned. The growing part of the stem is harvested for palm heart, which is eaten. Cutting the stem kills it, but peach palm clumps freely and produces more stems. Occasionally a plant will have a single trunk. One cultivar has few spines.

Care: Fast-growing peach palm flourishes in well-drained acidic or alkaline soil high in organic matter. It needs regular water and fertilizer. It does not tolerate drought, and it is especially sensitive to salt.

Recommended uses: This palm can serve as an impenetrable privacy barrier as well as a beautiful specimen plant surrounded only by lawn or a low groundcover.

Beccariophoenix madagascariensis
beh-kar-ee-o-FEE-nix mad-uh-gas-kar-ee-EN-sis

Giant windowpane palm

- **Size:** 35–45'H×15–20'W
- **Light:** Full sun
- **Water:** Moderate
- **Minimum temperature:** 30°F
- **Features:** Single-trunk feather-leaf palm

At a young age this Madagascar native has leaflets that stick together and form small gaps where they join the leaf stem. The fact that these gaps look like windowpanes spaced along the stem has given the plant its common name. A mature giant windowpane palm looks like a coconut palm, except that it has a fatter trunk (12 to 16 inches in diameter) covered in brown hairy fibers in its younger part. The leaves are light grassy green and can grow 15 feet long. The fruit is purplish brown.

Care: This palm, which grows at a moderate rate, does well in acidic to slightly alkaline soil that is well drained. It needs regular watering because it is not particularly drought-tolerant. It has little tolerance for salt. A young plant appreciates an extra dose of iron along with its regular feeding.

Recommended uses: Use giant windowpane palm for an effect similar to that provided by coconut palm. It is graceful as a specimen plant or in small groupings. This palm combines well with other tropical plants.

Giant windowpane palm

Bismarckia nobilis
biz-MARK-ee-uh NO-buh-lis

Bismarck palm

- **Size:** 40–50'H×20–25'W
- **Light:** Full sun
- **Water:** Drought tolerant to low
- **Minimum temperature:** 25–28°F
- **Features:** Single-trunk fan-leaf palm with green or bluish leaves

Bismarck palm

Bismarck palm comes from Madagascar, where it grows nearly 80 feet tall. In cultivation it is much shorter with a brownish trunk that is about 18 inches in diameter. The leaves, which measure 8 feet long, can be silvery blue or any of several shades of green. A plant is either male or female. A male must grow nearby for a female to produce fruits, which are dark brown.

Care: This palm is easy to care for and has no special nutrient needs. It is a moderate grower that succeeds in well-drained acidic or alkaline soil. Although the plant tolerates periods of wet or dry, it appreciates regular water. It has a slight salt tolerance. Plants that are bluish seem to be cold-hardier than green individuals.

Recommended uses: This stately palm is a large-scale plant that looks out of place in small areas. In a large open landscape it makes a dramatic statement. It works well as a specimen in a formal garden or with other plants in a lush tropical setting.

Borassus aethiopium
bor-ASS-us ee-thee-O-pee-um

Ronier palm

- **Size: 50–80'H×25–30'W**
- **Light: Full sun**
- **Water: Drought tolerant to low**
- **Minimum temperature: 28°F**
- **Features: Single-trunk fan-leaf palm with blackish leaf stems**

Ronier palm

A large palm from tropical Africa, ronier palm has a trunk to 3 feet thick that is usually covered in shiny black old leaf bases. The nearly circular leaves are deep green and measure 10 to 12 feet long. Sharp teeth line both margins of the leaf stems. It takes both a male and a female plant to produce fruit, which is the size of a softball.

Care: This palm prospers in well-drained acidic or alkaline soil. Regular water and fertilizer keep it healthy. It tolerates short periods of drought and has good salt tolerance. When the plant is young, it grows slowly, but at an intermediate age it speeds up until it starts flowering and then slows down again.

Recommended uses: Ronier palm is a big plant that demands a large open area or planting bed where it can become a canopy tree. It will swallow a small yard, overwhelm a small house, and look completely out of scale near compact plants. It works well in a formal or heavily planted tropical setting.

Brahea armata
bruh-HEE-uh ar-MAHT-uh

Blue hesper palm, Mexican blue palm

- **Size: 35–45'H×15–20'W**
- **Light: Full sun**
- **Water: Drought tolerant**
- **Minimum temperature: 25°F**
- **Features: Single-trunk fan-leaf palm with bluish leaves**

A native of Mexico and Baja California, blue hesper palm has a brownish trunk with a swollen base and a diameter of 18 inches or so. The 4- to 6-foot-long leaves vary from light silvery blue to blue-green. The cream-color flower clusters are quite ornamental: They extend out and nearly down to the ground, even on large specimens. The fruit is black.

Care: This drought-tolerant palm grows poorly when given too much water and does not appreciate wet Florida summers. A slow grower, it flourishes in well-drained soil that is somewhat alkaline to slightly acidic. The plant enjoys regular feeding, and it has some salt tolerance.

Recommended uses: With its enticing bluish foliage and dramatic flowering habit, hesper blue palm is a wonderful addition to a landscape that needs a large specimen plant. It is also a standout when surrounded by contrasting foliage.

Blue hesper palm

Brahea brandegeei
bruh-HEE-uh bran-DEE-jee-eye

San Jose hesper palm

- **Size: 30–40'H×10–12'W**
- **Light: Full sun**
- **Water: Drought tolerant to low**
- **Minimum temperature: 28°F**
- **Features: Single-trunk fan-leaf palm with small teeth on leaf stems**

San Jose hesper palm

This palm is from Baja Mexico, where it grows in canyons. Its 10- to 12-inch-thick trunk is covered in old leaf bases that form a crisscross pattern. The leaves, about 3 feet across, are medium green on top and light silver underneath. The leaf stems are armed with small teeth. The fruit is golden yellow to light brown.

Care: Slow-growing San Jose hesper palm thrives in well-drained alkaline to somewhat acidic soil. The plant does best with regular water and fertilizer, though it is drought tolerant when older. It has a slight salt tolerance.

Recommended uses: One of the smaller palms in its genus, San Jose hesper palm looks best planted in a grouping. It can be used as a stand-alone palm but comes alive in a planting bed with other foliage surrounding its base.

Brahea edulis
bruh-HEE-uh ED-yoo-lis
Guadalupe palm

- **Size: 30–40'H×10–15'W**
- **Light: Full sun**
- **Water: Drought tolerant to low**
- **Minimum temperature: 28°F**
- **Features: Single-trunk fan-leaf palm with small teeth on leaf stems**

Guadalupe palm

A stocky palm native to the island of Guadalupe off Baja California, this palm has a medium brown to gray trunk with a diameter of 12 to 16 inches. The light to medium green leaves, which form a half circle, measure up to 4 feet across. The leaf stems are armed with teeth, which disappear in some older individuals. The fruit is golden brown to almost black.
Care: Slow-growing Guadalupe palm needs well-drained alkaline to somewhat acidic soil. It does better in drier climates than in Florida, where it shows stress from the summer wet season. Regular feeding is sufficient for good growth. The plant has excellent drought tolerance and has some salt tolerance.
Recommended uses: Guadalupe palm makes a beautiful formal specimen either by itself or in a grouping. It is equally at home in a bed of tropical plants with contrasting foliage.

Butia capitata
BYOO-tee-uh kap-ih-TAHT-uh
Pindo palm

- **Size: 25–30'H×12–15'W**
- **Light: Full sun**
- **Water: Drought tolerant to low**
- **Minimum temperature: 25°F**
- **Features: Single-trunk feather-leaf palm with bluish leaves**

Pindo palm is native to southern Brazil and Uruguay, where it generally grows in open savannahs. The trunk, around 18 inches thick and naturally covered in old leaf bases, can be quite ornamental. The arching leaves are 6 to 10 feet long and vary from medium green to blue to almost whitish silver. The sweet edible fruit, yellow to reddish orange when ripe, is delicious.

A hybrid of pindo palm with queen palm, called butiagrus or mule palm, is a popular cold-hardy palm.
Care: Slow-growing pindo palm is not fussy about whether the soil is acidic or alkaline as long as it drains well. The plant has no special nutrient needs and is drought tolerant and somewhat salt tolerant. Its only limitation is that it does not do well in the extreme nighttime heat of South Florida.
Recommended uses: This palm is a standout whether you plant just one or several. It looks equally good standing by itself or as the focal point in a lush tropical bed.

Pindo palm

Calamus caryotoides
KAL-uh-mus kar-ee-oh-TOI-deez
Fishtail lawyer cane

- **Size: 25–40'H×6–10'W**
- **Light: Heavy to moderate shade**
- **Water: Moderate**
- **Minimum temperature: 32°F**
- **Features: Multitrunk feather-leaf vining palm with spines**

Fishtail lawyer cane

A member of the rattan palms, this Australian species is used more as an ornamental plant while others in the genus are harvested for their trunks, which are used to make furniture and other products. Some of those palms are nearing extinction from overharvesting. This densely clumping species has spiny trunks less than an inch thick. The short (just 1 foot long) leaves have backward-facing spines along the leaf stem to help the plant attach itself to anything it can climb. The dangling buff to nearly white fruit is ornamental.
Care: Given a shady spot and something to climb, this fast grower will take off as long as it has regular water and fertilizer. It prefers acidic soil that is humusy and well drained, but it doesn't tolerate drought or salt.
Recommended uses: Locate fishtail lawyer cane where you can see and enjoy its features up close. It needs support to ascend, so plant it where it can grow into a tree or onto a shaded trellis. Take care not to plant it where it can overwhelm smaller plantings.

Calyptrocalyx albertisianus
kuh-lip-tro-KAY-lix al-ber-tiss-ee-AHN-us

Sunset palm

- **Size:** 20–25'H×12–15'W
- **Light:** Moderate to light shade
- **Water:** Wet
- **Minimum temperature:** 32°F
- **Features:** Single-trunk feather-leaf palm with red new leaves

Sunset palm

This New Guinea native gets its common name from the brilliant red of its new leaves as they emerge. The arching foliage, which can grow 8 to 10 feet long, gradually turns medium green over a couple of weeks. The dark tan trunk is 6 to 10 inches in diameter.
Care: Sunset palm requires well-drained acidic soil containing some organic matter. It has no drought or salt tolerance. The plant grows at a moderate rate with regular water and fertilizer. Although moderate shade is best, the plant can tolerate light shade to full sun at maturity.
Recommended uses: Sunset palm is dazzling when the new leaves show off their marvelous color, but the tree does not look its best standing alone. Surround it with other lower-growing tropical plants, and leave room for an unobscured view of the periodic display of red foliage.

Calyptrocalyx hollrungii
kuh-lip-tro-KAY-lix hohl-ROONG-ee-eye

Hollrung palm

- **Size:** 8–10'H×4–6'W
- **Light:** Heavy to moderate shade
- **Water:** Wet
- **Minimum temperature:** 32°F
- **Features:** Multitrunk feather-leaf palm with deep red to maroon new leaves

A native of New Guinea, this densely clumping palm has trunks to an inch wide that are covered in old leaf bases. The 18-inch leaves can be undivided or lightly segmented. The newly emerging leaves are deep red to maroon; they gradually turn khaki green over a week or two.
Care: Provide humusy acidic soil that is well drained. The plant does not tolerate drought or exposure to salt. Regular water and fertilizer are mandatory for good growth, which tends to be slow.
Recommended uses: A beautiful palm like this should be planted in an intimate spot where it can be appreciated up close. It is one of the few palms that looks best as a solitary specimen. Also use it as an understory or patio plant.

Hollrung palm

Calyptrocalyx polyphyllus
kuh-lip-tro-KAY-lix pah-lee-FY-lus

Flame palm

- **Size:** 8–12'H×6–10'W
- **Light:** Heavy to moderate shade
- **Water:** Wet
- **Minimum temperature:** 32°F
- **Features:** Multitrunk feather-leaf palm with red new leaves

Flame palm; red new leaf (inset)

This New Guinea native is a relatively new species in cultivation. The clump of slender trunks 1 to 2 inches thick is airier than those of other multitrunk species in the genus. The new leaves are deep red with green veins; they turn deep emerald green as they mature. The 3- to 5-foot-long glossy leaves are divided into leaflets that end in a tapered extension called a drip tip. These many outstanding features give flame palm a special charm.
Care: This palm flourishes when grown in well-drained acidic soil and given regular fertilizer. It does not tolerate drought or salt. Water it regularly to avoid stressing it.
Recommended uses: Use flame palm alone or amid other plants—but locate it where you can enjoy its decorative features up close. As a specimen under a high-canopied tree, it's an attractive conversation piece. It also makes an effective screen when planted close together in a group.

Calyptrogyne ghiesbreghtiana
kuh-lip-TROH-jeye-nee gees-breg-tee-AHN-uh

Rat's tail palm

- **Size:** 4–6'H×4–6'W
- **Light:** Heavy shade
- **Water:** Wet
- **Minimum temperature:** 32°F
- **Features:** Single-trunk feather-leaf palm with pinkish new leaves

Rat's tail palm

This palm gets its common name from the single thin flower spike that looks like a rat's tail poking up through the leaves. Native to Central America, rat's tail palm has a trunk that grows underground, so the 3- to 4-foot-long leaves appear to emerge directly from the soil. The new leaves are pinkish and bear only a few irregularly spaced leaflets of varying widths.

Care: Providing ample shade and water are key to growing rat's tail palm successfully. The plant thrives on high humidity and regular water. It prefers humusy, well-drained acidic soil and does not tolerate salt. It has no special nutrient needs or disease problems.

Recommended uses: An intimate spot in a rain forest-style landscape allows this palm to show off its beauty. Use a grouping of rat's tail palms among other tropical foliage plants to produce the feel and splendor of an understory rain forest.

Carpentaria acuminata
kar-pen-TAR-ee-uh uh-kyoo-min-AH-tuh

Carpentaria palm

- **Size:** 50–60'H×10–12'W
- **Light:** Full sun
- **Water:** Low to moderate
- **Minimum temperature:** 30°F
- **Features:** Single-trunk feather-leaf palm with crownshaft

Carpentaria palm, which grows along stream beds in its native Australia, has a tapering smooth gray trunk 6 to 8 inches in diameter. The crownshaft and the beautifully arching 8- to 10-foot-long leaves are deep green. The plant produces abundant crimson fruit.

Care: The plant does well in acidic or alkaline soil with some organic matter mixed in. It thrives in wet conditions but has some drought tolerance. This fast grower needs only regular fertilizer. It does not tolerate salt, and it endures only short exposure to temperatures below 32°F. Its foliage is often tattered by wind.

Recommended uses: A graceful rounded crown atop a tapering trunk and masses of crimson fruit make this plant an elegant addition to any garden. A grouping of several creates a wonderful canopy below which other tropical plants can flourish. For a spectacular evening effect, consider using the plant where the sunset will silhouette it.

Carpentaria palm

Carpoxylon macrospermum
kar-PAHX-ih-lahn mak-ro-SPER-mum

Carpoxylon palm

- **Size:** 45–60'H×12–15'W
- **Light:** Full sun
- **Water:** Moderate
- **Minimum temperature:** 30°F
- **Features:** Single-trunk feather-leaf palm with crownshaft

Carpoxylon palm

Once thought to be extinct, this palm was recently rediscovered in Vanuatu, and seeds were distributed throughout the world to ensure its survival. The mature trunk bulges at the base and tapers to about 12 inches across at the upper section. The trunk is deep green below the crownshaft, which is also green. The lower portion of the trunk turns gray as it ages. The leaves match the crownshaft in color, are beautifully arched, and reach 6 to 8 feet long. The fruit is the size of a small bird egg.

Care: Moderately fast-growing carpoxylon palm is easy to care for. It needs well-drained soil, which can be either acidic or alkaline. The plant thrives on regular water and fertilizer. It tolerates short dry periods and a small amount of salt. Although it prefers some shade when young, it grows well in full sun after the first couple of years.

Recommended uses: With its bulbous base, green upper trunk, and arched leaves, carpoxylon palm displays a beautiful form whether planted alone or in a grouping. Avoid planting other plants around the base that detract from the palm's beauty.

Caryota gigas
kar-ee-O-tuh JEYE-gus
Giant fishtail palm

- **Size: 50–70'H×25–35'W**
- **Light: Full sun**
- **Water: Low to moderate**
- **Minimum temperature: 28°F**
- **Features: Single-trunk bipinnate-leaf palm**

Giant fishtail palm

This massive palm is native to Southern China and Laos, where it grows on mountainsides at an elevation of 4,000 to 5,000 feet. Its grayish or tan trunk is 3 feet wide. The stiffly upright emerald green leaves are triangular and can reach 20 feet long and 10 feet wide. Because it is a monocarpic palm, once it finishes fruiting it dies. The dying process can take up to three years, and the overall lifespan of the palm can be 25 to 30 years. The ripe fruits are red.

Care: This palm grows in full sun at a moderate rate. The exception is South Florida, where it grows much more slowly in the summer nighttime heat. It can take either acidic or alkaline soil. Like all species in the genus, it likes moderately wet soil. It also has little salt tolerance. Keep the plant well watered and fertilized, and it will grow robustly.

Recommended uses: Giant fishtail palm turns into what looks like a huge tree fern. It requires a large landscape to accommodate it, to provide the proper scale, and to allow space so you can stand back and appreciate its form.

Caryota mitis
kar-ee-O-tuh MY-tis
Clumping fishtail palm

- **Size: 15–20'H×10–15'W**
- **Light: Light shade to full sun**
- **Water: Low to moderate**
- **Minimum temperature: 32°F**
- **Features: Multitrunk bipinnate-leaf palm**

Native to India and the Philippines, clumping fishtail palm is common throughout palm-growing regions of the world. The trunks of this densely clumping palm are 4 to 6 inches in diameter, and the light green leaves grow to 8 feet long. Once a trunk begins to flower from the top down, it will die in about two years, but seedlings often take the place of dying stems. The fruit matures to either red or black. Handle the fruit with care because it contains a strong skin irritant.

Care: Clumping fishtail palm does well in wet acidic or alkaline soil. Regular water and fertilizer keep this palm growing relatively fast. The plant does not tolerate salt. The leaves are deeper green when the plant is grown in light shade rather than full sun. Indoors it requires bright light and high humidity to do well.

Recommended uses: This palm can be grown indoors where it makes a striking houseplant. In the landscape, plant it singly as a specimen or in a group for a screen that has a coarse, ferny texture.

Clumping fishtail palm

Caryota urens
kar-ee-O-tuh YOOR-enz
Toddy fishtail palm

- **Size: 40–50'H×15–20'W**
- **Light: Full sun**
- **Water: Low to moderate**
- **Minimum temperature: 28–30°F**
- **Features: Single-trunk bipinnate-leaf palm**

Toddy fishtail palm

Toddy fishtail palm is a widely cultivated palm that comes from India and Sri Lanka. It has a gray trunk that can grow up to 18 inches thick. The medium to deep green triangular leaves, growing to 12 feet long, droop at the end. The black fruit contains one to three seeds. In some parts of the world, sap from the flower is collected to make an alcoholic beverage or toddy.

Care: The more water and fertilizer that you provide for this palm, the faster it grows. It prefers some wetness but tolerates dry conditions. The plant grows equally well in acidic or alkaline soil, preferably with some organic matter mixed in. It has little tolerance for salt. Forms that originate from higher elevations are cold hardier than ones from lower elevations.

Recommended uses: Toddy fishtail palm looks best planted in a grouping in an open area where the cluster forms an attractive silhouette against the sky. Plant a low groundcover underneath the palms to tie them to the surrounding landscape.

Ceroxylon quindiuense
seh-RAHX-ih-lahn keen-dee-oo-EN-see

Andean wax palm

- **Size: 50–70'H×15–20'W**
- **Light: Full sun**
- **Water: Moderate**
- **Minimum temperature: 28°F**
- **Features: Single-trunk feather-leaf palm**

Andean wax palm

Andean wax palm is the world's tallest palm (not counting the vining rattan palms that can grow 300 feet long). In its native habitat in the Andes in Columbia, the plant grows to 200 feet tall. Such plants must be ancient considering this palm's slow growth rate. The leaves are up to 15 feet long and bear pendent leaflets that are dark green on top and silver underneath.

Care: You'll need patience to germinate this palm from seed. It is slow to emerge from the soil. It does not tolerate the hot summer nights of Florida but does well in the parts of California where summer nights are cooler. Andean wax palm requires well-drained soil as well as regular water and fertilizer. It has a slight tolerance for drought and none for salt.

Recommended uses: This palm can make a beautiful canopy by itself or in a grouping if you have the patience to wait for it to grow to its potential height. It is also visually pleasing as a young plant on its own or amid other foliage plants.

Chamaedorea adscendens
kah-mee-DOR-ee-uh ad-SEND-enz

Velvet palm

- **Size: 2–3'H×1–2'W**
- **Light: Heavy to moderate shade**
- **Water: Moderate**
- **Minimum temperature: 30°F**
- **Features: Single-trunk feather-leaf palm**

A diminutive plant from Belize, this palm gets its common name from the velvety appearance of its deep bluish green leaves. This is one of the smallest of all palms. The trunk is less than an inch in diameter, and each leaf—including the leaf stem—less than a foot long. Occasionally the leaves are whole rather than divided into leaflets, and they look like fish tails. The fruit is black.

Care: This moderate grower prefers well-drained alkaline soil with a little organic matter mixed in. Velvet palm is a shade lover with no tolerance for salt. Regular water and fertilizer fulfill its basic needs. Indoors it needs bright light and high humidity.

Recommended uses: Use velvet palm in masses as a groundcover in a shaded area. An individual plant is lost in the landscape, but a large grouping creates a wonderfully soft texture under the canopy of palm trees or other foliage plants. This little palm is also a good potted plant for indoors.

Velvet palm

Chamaedorea cataractarum
kah-mee-DOR-ee-uh kat-uh-RAK-tuh-rum

Cat palm

- **Size: 6–8'H×6–8'W**
- **Light: Moderate shade to full sun**
- **Water: Moderate**
- **Minimum temperature: 30°F**
- **Features: Multitrunk feather-leaf palm**

Cat palm

This palm with no visible trunk comes from Mexico, where it grows along streams and riverbanks. The 4- to 6-foot-long leaves are deep green. The leaf color intensifies and the leaves get longer in the shade than in full sun. The black fruit is hidden under the dense foliage.

Care: Considering that cat palm grows along streams, it stands to reason that it does best under moist conditions. It prefers well-drained alkaline to slightly acidic soil. The plant grows at a moderate rate and has a low tolerance for salt. If you grow this palm in full sun, give it additional fertilizer to maintain its deep green color. When grown indoors cat palm needs a lot of light and high humidity; it is highly susceptible to spider mite and mealybug infestations.

Recommended uses: Cat palm's beauty lies in its lush deep green foliage. Use the plant where that asset stands out—around water features, for example, where it looks completely at home. It is attractive in informal groupings and provides an excellent privacy screen. It makes an attractive houseplant if kept moist.

Chamaedorea elegans
kah-mee-DOR-ee-uh EL-eh-gunz
Parlor palm

- **Size:** 5–8'H×2–3'W
- **Light:** Heavy shade
- **Water:** Low to moderate
- **Minimum temperature:** 30°F
- **Features:** Single-trunk feather-leaf palm

Parlor palm

This palm has graced the parlors of elegant homes since the 1800s. Native to Belize and Mexico, it has a light green trunk less than an inch thick. The leaves are light to medium green and generally no more than 2 feet long. The fruit is shiny black.

Care: Parlor palm thrives in well-drained acidic or alkaline soil that is high in organic matter. The plant does not tolerate salt. It grows at a slow to moderate rate and has no special nutrient needs. Shade is essential: The foliage may burn and the plant declines if given too much sun. As with most palms grown indoors, spider mites can be an occasional problem.

Recommended uses: This is one of the best palms for indoor use. Its slow growth and small stature make it an excellent long-term potted plant. Parlor palm is generally grown with multiple stems in a container to give it fullness. Whether used indoors or in the landscape, parlor palm adds a graceful elegance to an area. Outdoors use a grouping because a solitary plant may not make an impression.

Chamaedorea ernesti-augustii
kah-mee-DOR-ee-uh er-nest-ee-aw-GUS-tee-eye
Tuna tail palm

- **Size:** 6–10'H×2–3'W
- **Light:** Heavy shade
- **Water:** Moderate
- **Minimum temperature:** 30°F
- **Features:** Single-trunk feather-leaf palm with undivided leaves

This palm's common name comes from its leaf shape, which resembles a fish tail. A native of southern Mexico and Central America, the plant has a trunk that is less than an inch in diameter and light to medium green leaves to 18 inches long. Stilt roots (aboveground brace roots) that become anchored in the soil and help support the palm as it gets taller can develop in a high-humidity setting. The fruit is shiny black.

Care: Tuna tail palm, which grows at a moderate rate, succeeds in acidic or alkaline soil that contains some organic matter. It does not tolerate full sun. Never expose the plant to salt air or allow it to dry out.

Recommended uses: As a specimen, tuna tail palm adds whimsy to a landscape, but it stands out better when several are planted in a grouping. It adds contrast to a landscape because its leaves are generally a lighter green than those of most other plants.

Tuna tail palm

Chamaedorea metallica
kah-mee-DOR-ee-uh meh-TAL-ik-uh
Miniature fishtail palm

- **Size:** 4–6'H×2–3'W
- **Light:** Heavy to light shade
- **Water:** Moderate
- **Minimum temperature:** 30°F
- **Features:** Single-trunk feather-leaf palm usually with undivided leaves

Miniature fishtail palm

This Mexican native gets its botanical name from its leaves, which are deep bluish green with a metallic sheen. Occasionally the foot-long leaves are segmented, but usually they are undivided and shaped like a fish tail. The dark green trunk is only ½ inch thick. The flower stalks are bright orange and the fruit is black.

Care: Slow-growing miniature fishtail palm thrives in well-drained alkaline to somewhat acidic soil. It does not tolerate drought, salt, or full sun and has no special nutrient needs or disease problems. If the plant gets too tall and spindly you can air-layer it (roots develop easily); however do this only as a last resort because air-layering kills the original stem.

Recommended uses: Use miniature fishtail palm as a groundcover, grow it in large groupings in beds for a glistening lush look, or situate it among other foliage plants to show off its contrasting form. It is one of the best palms to use indoors: Plant three or five in a pot to add fullness to the container.

Chamaedorea microspadix
kah-mee-DOR-ee-uh my-kro-SPAY-dix

Hardy bamboo palm

- **Size:** 8–12'H×8–10'W
- **Light:** Heavy to moderate shade
- **Water:** Moderate
- **Minimum temperature:** 23°F
- **Features:** Multitrunk feather-leaf palm with scarlet fruit

Hardy bamboo palm

Hardy bamboo palm survives unscathed at temperatures into the low 20s. A native of Mexico it is a loose to densely clumping palm with green trunks less than an inch thick. The leaves, up to 2 feet long, are dark green with a soft silver cast. The ripe fruit, which remains on the plant for several weeks, is scarlet.

Care: Moderately fast-growing hardy bamboo palm is easy to care for. It can take either acidic or alkaline soil as long as it drains well. It needs regular water and fertilizer and does not tolerate drought or salt very well. The plant tolerates light shade, although it turns lighter green in shade. Spider mites can be troublesome when the plant is grown indoors, where it needs bright light and high humidity.

Recommended uses: With its red fruit and soft texture, hardy bamboo palm serves as a colorful and graceful focal point. It looks best surrounded by other foliage plants, and it also makes a good screen. This palm can also be grown indoors.

Chamaedorea oblongata
kah-mee-DOR-ee-uh ahb-long-GAHT-uh

Cauqui palm

- **Size:** 8–10'H×3–4'W
- **Light:** Heavy shade
- **Water:** Moderate
- **Minimum temperature:** 30°F
- **Features:** Single-trunk feather-leaf palm

Cauqui palm is native to southern Mexico and Central America. The dark green trunk is about an inch in diameter. The leaves, growing 2 feet or longer, develop into glossy deep green fronds. The leaflets are cupped, adding to the plant's beauty. The fruit is shiny black.

Care: This moderate grower thrives in well-drained soil that is either acidic or alkaline. The plant needs regular water and fertilizer. It has no special nutrient requirements, but some organic matter in the soil helps it look its best. Cauqui palm does not perform well in full sun. It tolerates only the slightest amount of salt air and is intolerant of drought. No disease problems affect it.

Recommended uses: With its glossy dark green leaves at eye level, cauqui palm commands attention as an understory planting. It looks especially good in a group of several plants of staggered heights. Its small stature and tolerance for low light make it an excellent indoor potted palm. Provide it with a bright location out of direct sun indoors.

Cauqui palm

Chamaedorea radicalis
kah-mee-DOR-ee-uh rad-ih-KAL-iss

Dwarf bamboo palm

- **Size:** 4–6'H×3–5'W
- **Light:** Heavy to moderate shade
- **Water:** Moderate
- **Minimum temperature:** 25°F
- **Features:** Single-trunk feather-leaf palm

Dwarf bamboo palm

This relatively cold-hardy native of Mexico usually has a trunk that grows belowground, but at times it develops an inch-thick stem that reaches 10 to 12 feet tall. The leaves, to 3 feet long, are medium to dark green. The fruit is orangish red.

Care: Dwarf bamboo palm succeeds in well-drained acidic or alkaline soil, preferably containing some organic matter. The plant, which grows at a moderate rate, needs regular water and fertilizer. It is not drought-tolerant and only slightly salt-tolerant. Although it tolerates light shade, in that level of shade its foliage will be lighter green.

Recommended uses: Plant a grouping of dwarf bamboo palm under a tree canopy and add a contrasting low groundcover. As a single specimen this palm gets lost among other plants. It makes an acceptable indoor plant, although other palms in the genus are better for that purpose.

Chamaedorea seifrizii
kah-mee-DOR-ee-uh seye-FRITZ-ee-eye

Bamboo palm

- **Size: 8–10'H×5–7'W**
- **Light: Heavy to light shade**
- **Water: Moderate**
- **Minimum temperature: 30°F**
- **Features: Multitrunk feather-leaf palm**

Bamboo palm

Frequently grown as an indoor plant, bamboo palm is native to Mexico, Belize, Guatemala, and Honduras and has different leaf forms depending on the plant's origin. The leaflets may be narrow or wide, and they range in color from medium to deep green. The green trunks are nearly an inch in diameter. The fruit is shiny black. Commercial growers sometimes grow bamboo palm in full sun to make the plants dense and full and then move them into shade to turn them dark green and feathery for indoor use.

Care: Moderately fast-growing bamboo palm does best in well-drained soil with some organic matter mixed in. Soil can be either acidic or alkaline. It needs regular water and fertilizer. The plant has a slight salt tolerance. It prefers shady conditions, although it tolerates bright light in the garden if gradually acclimated to it.

Recommended uses: This palm creates a beautiful silhouette against a light-colored wall in deep shade. It has few equals indoors, where it requires medium light and high humidity for best growth.

Chamaedorea tepejilote
kah-mee-DOR-ee-uh tep-ay-hee-LO-tee

Pacaya palm

- **Size: 10–20'H×5–20'W**
- **Light: Heavy to moderate shade**
- **Water: Moderate**
- **Minimum temperature: 30°F**
- **Features: Single- or multitrunk feather-leaf palm**

Pacaya palm is usually single trunked, but some develop a clump that may reach 20 feet tall and wide. The trunks range from 1 to 3 inches wide. The 3- to 6-foot-long gracefully arching leaves are medium green and typically have a yellow stripe running up the base and along the midrib. The fruit is shiny black. The plant is widely cultivated in Central America and Columbia for the male flower clusters; they are collected just before they open and then cooked and eaten.

Care: Fast-growing pacaya palm wants humusy, well-drained acidic or alkaline soil. The plant needs regular water and has no special nutrient needs or disease problems. It has little tolerance for salt or drought.

Recommended uses: Plant a small group of pacaya palms of varying heights under a high tree canopy, then underplant with other shorter plants to create a lush tropical landscape at several levels.

Pacaya palm

Chamaerops humilis
kah-MEE-rahps HYOO-mih-lis

European fan palm

- **Size: 15–20'H×20–25'W**
- **Light: Full sun**
- **Water: Drought tolerant**
- **Minimum temperature: 16°F**
- **Features: Multitrunk fan-leaf palm**

European fan palm

Native to the Mediterranean region, European fan palm is a variable species that normally forms multiple trunks and rarely just one. The trunks reach 8 inches in diameter and are generally covered in brownish fibers from old leaf bases. The semicircular leaves, to 2 feet across, range in color from olive to blue-green to silvery blue. The golden yellow to almost brown fruit hangs in dense clusters just under the leaves.

Care: Although this slow-growing palm does well in Florida, the best specimens are found in dry-summer climates such as in California. The plant is not particular about soil requirements other than good drainage and has no special nutrient needs or disease problems. Its drought tolerance is excellent and its salt tolerance very good.

Recommended uses: European fan palm becomes sculptural when it's planted as a specimen. Because its overall shape is a rounded mound, it also works as a formal element in a garden. Use it in large planters by buildings, walls, or walkways, or combine it with succulents to create contrast.

Chambeyronia macrocarpa
shahm-bay-RO-nee-uh mak-ro-KARP-uh

Red feather palm

- **Size: 25–35'H×10–15'W**
- **Light: Light shade to full sun**
- **Water: Moderate**
- **Minimum temperature: 30°F**
- **Features: Single-trunk feather-leaf palm with crownshaft and red new leaves**

Red feather palm

A native of New Caledonia, red feather palm has a trunk to 10 inches in diameter topped with glossy dark green leaves that can reach 12 feet long. Most of the leaves emerge brilliant red (some never do), then turn dark green in a week or two. The crownshaft and upper trunk are dark green, and the lower trunk grayish. The ripe fruit is deep red.
Care: Red feather palm, which grows at a moderate pace, is equally happy in well-drained acidic or alkaline soil with some organic matter mixed in. The plant needs regular water and has no special nutrient requirements. It has a slight salt tolerance. Although this palm tolerates full sun, it is most at home in light shade.
Recommended uses: A graceful palm that periodically develops a bright red new leaf is a standout in any garden. Use it individually or in a small group. Plant it near the front edge of a planting bed under a canopy of light shade.

Clinostigma samoense
kleye-no-STIG-muh sah-mo-EN-see

Samoan palm

- **Size: 40–60'H×20–25'W**
- **Light: Full sun**
- **Water: Moderate**
- **Minimum temperature: 32°F**
- **Features: Single-trunk feather-leaf palm with crownshaft**

Samoa is home to this exotic palm, which has a beautifully ringed trunk about a foot wide. The trunk is waxy green in its upper section, and the crownshaft is waxy light green to yellowish green. The medium to deep green leaves grow as long as 20 feet and develop a gentle arch. The leaflets appear nearly pendent as they droop from the central leaf stem.
Care: Fast-growing Samoan palm prefers well-drained acidic soil, though it tolerates some alkalinity. It is not drought-tolerant; provide regular water. The plant also needs regular feeding. It tolerates an occasional brief cold snap to near freezing but generally is intolerant of cold. Its salt tolerance is fair.
Recommended uses: This palm is the epitome of grace. A single tree makes a beautiful silhouette against a tropical sky, and several grouped are equally attractive. Samoan palm grows well with plants around its base, but keep its crown open to the sky. Also avoid crowding it with other tall trees.

Samoan palm

Coccothrinax argentata
ko-ko-THRY-nax ar-jen-TAHT-uh

Silver thatch palm

- **Size: 12–15'H×5–7'W**
- **Light: Full sun**
- **Water: Drought tolerant**
- **Minimum temperature: 28°F**
- **Features: Single-trunk fan-leaf palm with silvery leaf undersides**

Silver thatch palm

Silver thatch palm is native to Florida and the Bahamas. The 3- to 4-inch-diameter trunk is light to medium gray. The nearly circular leaves, 2 to 3 feet wide, are dark green on top and pale silver underneath. The fruit is purplish black.
Care: A very slow grower, silver thatch palm does best in well-drained alkaline soil that is sandy or rocky. It is a drought-tolerant palm that requires little supplemental water except in arid climates. It has excellent salt tolerance and no special fertilizer requirements. Poor drainage and overwatering are the sources of most problems associated with this palm.
Recommended uses: Silver thatch palm looks best in a grouping. The contrast between the dark green leaf tops and the pale silver undersides as the leaves dance in the breeze makes this palm a visual delight. It looks great alone or with short groundcover plants around its base.

Coccothrinax barbadensis
ko-ko-THRY-nax bar-buh-DEN-sis

Barbados palm

- **Size: 35–45'H×6–8'W**
- **Light: Light shade to full sun**
- **Water: Low to moderate**
- **Minimum temperature: 30°F**
- **Features: Single-trunk fan-leaf palm with silver leaf undersides**

Barbados palm

Native to the Lesser Antilles, this palm is one of the tallest growers in its genus. The light gray trunk has a diameter of 4 to 5 inches; the younger portion is wrapped with fine fibers that are part of the old leaf bases. The 3-foot diameter leaves are medium to dark green on top and light silver underneath. The fruit is black.

Care: Slow-growing Barbados palm does best in well-drained neutral to alkaline soil. The plant has some drought tolerance but prefers regular water. It has no special fertilizer needs, and its salt tolerance is good. Although it tolerates light shade, it looks best in full sun. Mealybugs occasionally attack the emerging new growth, but you can control them with a light horticultural oil spray.

Recommended uses: As with most palms in this genus, Barbados palm looks best when planted in multiples of several at staggered heights. They make an acceptable display planted on their own but look better in a bed with other plants growing underneath them.

Coccothrinax borhidiana
ko-ko-THRY-nax bor-hid-ee-AN-uh

Borhidi palm

- **Size: 8–12'H×4–6'W**
- **Light: Full sun**
- **Water: Drought tolerant**
- **Minimum temperature: 30°F**
- **Features: Single-trunk fan-leaf palm with persistent skirt of old leaves**

Borhidi palm comes from a small area on the north coast of Cuba, where it grows in sharp limestone. A petticoat of old dead leaves covers the 3- to 4-inch-diameter trunk. Loosely knit fibers create a slightly hairy look among the new leaves, which have very short leaf stems. The circular leaves are dark green on top and silver underneath. The fruit is purple.

Care: This palm needs extremely well-drained alkaline soil that is rocky or sandy. It does not tolerate soil that can hold a lot of moisture. Light feeding with regular palm food is all that is needed for this slow grower. Although the plant is native to sea cliffs, its salt tolerance surprisingly is only fair.

Recommended uses: A stocky but highly ornamental plant, borhidi palm demands a sunny space near the front of a planting bed, where it can be closely viewed. Plant several in a bed surrounded by short groundcover plants.

Borhidi palm

Coccothrinax crinita
ko-ko-THRY-nax kreye-NEET-uh

Old man palm

- **Size: 15–20'H×6–8'W**
- **Light: Full sun**
- **Water: Low to moderate**
- **Minimum temperature: 30°F**
- **Features: Single-trunk fan-leaf palm with hairy trunk**

Old man palm; trunk fibers (inset)

Old man palm is native to Cuba. Its loose, hairy fibers from old leaf bases cover the entire 6- to 8-inch-thick trunk, making it resemble an old man's long beard. The fibers are light tan to golden yellow. In especially old specimens they fall off, providing a view of the gray trunk. The circular 3- to 4-foot-wide leaves are medium green on top and greenish silver underneath. The fruit is light lavender.

Care: This very slow-growing palm isn't fussy about whether the soil is acidic or alkaline as long as it drains well. The plant appreciates regular water, and its salt tolerance is low. Manganese deficiency is an occasional problem.

Recommended uses: Locate old man palm where you can enjoy it up close. Admirers will undoubtedly want to stroke its beard. It looks best—as either a specimen or in a group—near the edge of a planting bed where you can easily see the hairy fibers.

Coccothrinax miraguama
ko-ko-THRY-nax meer-uh-GWAH-muh
Miraguama palm

- Size: 25–30'H×6–8'W
- Light: Full sun
- Water: Low to moderate
- Minimum temperature: 30°F
- Features: Single-trunk fan-leaf palm with silvery leaf undersides

Miraguama palm

This native of Cuba is divided into four subspecies. The main differences among them are the thickness of the fibers on the leaf bases that cover the trunk and the stiffness of the leaves. The 4- to 6-inch-thick trunk is covered with a mesh of woven fibers on all but the oldest part, which is gray. The circular leaves, 2 to 3 feet across, are dark green on top and silver underneath. The fruit is black.
Care: A faster grower than most other species in the genus, miraguama palm prefers well-drained alkaline to neutral soil. The plant has no special nutrient needs. It has fair salt and drought tolerance.
Recommended uses: A grouping of several miraguama palms in a landscape can be quite dramatic. This palm looks best in a planting bed with shorter flowering or foliage plants underneath it. Mix it in with taller feather palms to add a new dimension to the landscape.

Coccothrinax spissa
ko-ko-THRY-nax SPIS-uh
Guano palm

- Size: 25–30'H×8–10'W
- Light: Full sun
- Water: Low to moderate
- Minimum temperature: 30°F
- Features: Single-trunk fan-leaf palm generally with a bulge in the trunk

In the wild in its native Dominican Republic, guano palm is recognizable by a distinct swelling or bulge in its smooth gray trunk. The bulge can be 2 feet thick; the rest of the trunk is 8 to 12 inches in diameter. In cultivation the trunk may show only a slight bulge but is extremely stocky from top to bottom. The nearly circular leaves, measuring 4 feet across, are medium to dark green on top and silver underneath. The fruit is purplish black.
Care: Guano palm does best in well-drained alkaline to slightly acidic soils. The plant has a moderate growth rate and rarely shows nutrient deficiencies. It tolerates some drought and some salt.
Recommended uses: With its bulging trunk and well-rounded crown of leaves, guano palm is an eyecatching addition to the landscape. Use it as a specimen or plant several in a grouping. It works well in planting beds surrounded by other plants.

Guano palm

Cocos nucifera
KO-kohs noo-SIF-er-uh
Coconut palm

- Size: 60–100'H×20–30'W
- Light: Full sun
- Water: Low to moderate
- Minimum temperature: 32°F
- Features: Single-trunk feather-leaf palm

Coconut palm

This is the most recognizable palm in the world. Travel brochures for exotic destinations feature coconut palm, which has become a symbol of the tropics. Its origin is unknown because it has been cultivated and used by indigenous people throughout the world for centuries. The leading theory is that it is native to the islands of the South Pacific. Many people are surprised to learn that coconut palm is not native to the Americas but was introduced by the Spanish during their conquest of the New World. The coconut itself is a beautifully packaged food source that was easily stored and eaten during long voyages back to Spain.

Cultivated varieties of coconut palm have names such as 'Malayan Dwarf', 'Fiji Dwarf', 'Panama Tall', 'Jamaican Tall', and 'Red Spicata'. All are similar in appearance; each name merely refers to the variety's place of origin and growth habit. The main distinction is height. Tall types reach heights of 100 feet or more and dwarfs 60 feet or so.
(continued)

Coconut palm *(continued)*

Some coconut palm trees have bulging bases while others do not. Trunk diameters vary from 10 to 18 inches at the base but consistently remain 10 to 12 inches in diameter from approximately 6 feet above the

Coconut palm fruits

ground on up. The trunk is gray to tan with an interesting pattern where the old leaves fell off. The leaves can reach a length of 15 feet; the leaflets usually spread out in a single plane, although sometimes they droop. Coconuts hang in clusters under and among the leaf bases. The immature fruit can range in color from green to yellow to red, but all coconuts turn brown eventually.

This species is the most economically important palm in the world. Many indigenous people use every part of the tree. The coconut fruit is a nutritious source of food and drink. Palm oil is produced from the edible part of the coconut. The leaves are used for roofing thatch and woven into wall partitions as well as baskets, hats, and all sorts of everyday household items. Coconut wood, particularly the outer part of the trunk, is cut and used for flooring and other construction projects. The wood flooring has become a popular product throughout the world, and furniture made from the wood is showing up in stores as well.

Care: Lethal yellowing disease is the main problem associated with coconut palm. The disease has ravaged the trees in Florida and in other parts of the world. Resistant varieties such as 'Malayan Dwarf' and Maypan Hybrids have been introduced with mixed success. Coconut palm is still heavily cultivated in Florida, and lethal yellowing infects a small percentage of the coconut palms there yearly. The tree has excellent salt tolerance as well as good drought tolerance. With regular water and fertilizer it grows quickly and robustly. The plant grows best in well-drained alkaline to neutral soil but it tolerates acidic conditions.

Coconut palm

Recommended uses: As a specimen, coconut palm is a picture of beauty. In a grouping of several it provides grace and casual elegance to a tropical landscape. It looks just as good with nothing around its trunk as it does with tropical plants growing at its base.

Coconut palm seedlings

Copernicia alba
ko-per-NISS-ee-uh AHL-buh
Caranday palm

- **Size: 35–40'H×10–12'W**
- **Light: Full sun**
- **Water: Low to moderate**
- **Minimum temperature: 25°F**
- **Features: Single-trunk fan-leaf palm with large teeth on leaf stems**

Caranday palm

Caranday palm is native to southern Brazil, Bolivia, Paraguay, and Argentina. In younger plants the leaves can be silvery to light blue, but generally they turn grayish green with a silver underside as they age. The trunk tends to be smoother when older. The fruit is black. This palm is quite similar in appearance to its relative carnauba wax palm. However, caranday palm has wider leaf segments than carnauba wax palm, and it also holds its leaves more tightly to the crown.

Care: This moderate grower does well in well-drained alkaline to slightly acidic soil. The plant prefers regular water but tolerates periods of drought or wet soil conditions. It has some salt tolerance. Potassium deficiency can occasionally be a problem; counteract it with a fertilizer high in slow-release potassium.

Recommended uses: Caranday palm looks best when several are planted in a group.

Copernicia baileyana
ko-per-NISS-ee-uh bay-lee-AHN-uh
Bailey palm

- **Size: 40–45'H×15–20'W**
- **Light: Full sun**
- **Water: Low to moderate**
- **Minimum temperature: 28°F**
- **Features: Single-trunk fan-leaf palm with black teeth on leaf stems**

Bailey palm

This palm native to Cuba is named after Liberty Hyde Bailey, a famous horticulturist and palm taxonomist who lived in the first half of the 20th century. In older plants the trunk is smooth whitish gray and 2 feet in diameter. The circular dark grayish green leaves measure 5 to 6 feet wide. The leaf stem margins are black and have regularly spaced teeth. The fruit is brown to black.

Care: Slow-growing Bailey palm prefers alkaline to neutral soil that is well drained. The plant tolerates seasonal flooding as well as short periods of drought but does best with regular water. It has some salt tolerance. Feed it regularly with palm food.

Recommended uses: This large palm needs a spacious open area to show off its features. Several Bailey palms in a cluster are absolutely stunning. It also makes a beautiful specimen when planted alone.

Copernicia hospita
ko-per-NISS-ee-uh HAHS-pit-uh
Cuban wax palm

- **Size: 15–20'H×12–15'W**
- **Light: Full sun**
- **Water: Low to moderate**
- **Minimum temperature: 28°F**
- **Features: Single-trunk fan-leaf palm with silvery or green leaves**

As you might expect from its common name, this palm is a native of Cuba. Its 10- to 14-inch-diameter trunk is often covered in old leaf bases. Older plants develop a smooth gray trunk in the older portion. The leaves, measuring about 4 feet wide, are generally circular and range from bright green to bluish silver. The color is due to wax that covers the leaf on both sides. The leaf stem edges are armed with teeth. The fruit is black.

Care: Very slow-growing Cuban wax palm does well in alkaline to slightly acidic soil that is well drained. During the rainy season in its native habitat it can sit in standing water for several months at a time. It is fairly drought-tolerant as well. A potassium deficiency can occur but is easily rectified with a slow-release potassium fertilizer. The plant's salt tolerance is good.

Recommended uses: Cuban wax palm is a beautiful landscape addition, either as a specimen or in a grouping. Its ornamental value increases when you use it with other *Copernicia* species.

Cuban wax palm

Copernicia macroglossa
ko-per-NISS-ee-uh mak-ro-GLOSS-uh
Cuban petticoat palm

- **Size: 20–25'H×12–15'W**
- **Light: Full sun**
- **Water: Low to moderate**
- **Minimum temperature: 28°F**
- **Features: Single-trunk fan-leaf palm with persistent skirt of old leaves**

Cuban petticoat palm

This palm native to Cuba is named for the petticoat of old leaves that it maintains as the leaves age. The trunk is 8 to 10 inches thick but is visible only in taller, more mature specimens or if the petticoat of leaves is removed. Medium green leaves form a half-circle and are held close to the trunk. The outer edges of the leaves may be armed with small teeth. The fruit is black.

Care: Very slow-growing Cuban petticoat palm flourishes in well-drained alkaline to slightly acidic soil. It tolerates wet or dry conditions but does best with regular water. A potassium deficiency can occur, but regular feeding with a fertilizer containing slow-release potassium should prevent the problem from developing. The plant has excellent salt tolerance.

Recommended uses: Even at a young age, Cuban petticoat palm makes an extraordinary addition to the landscape. As a specimen it's a natural focal point. It is also attractive when several are planted in a group.

Copernicia prunifera
ko-per-NISS-ee-uh proon-IF-er-uh
Carnauba wax palm

- Size: 35–40'H×12–15'W
- Light: Full sun
- Water: Low to moderate
- Minimum temperature: 25°F
- Features: Single-trunk fan-leaf palm with big teeth on leaf stems

Carnauba wax palm

Carnauba wax palm is a native of Brazil, where it can grow to nearly 60 feet tall. Its common name refers to the carnauba wax that is extracted from the leaves and is used in various polishes, cosmetics, and food. The trunk is about 10 inches in diameter; the older portion is covered with knobby leaf base scars that create a spiral pattern. The circular gray-green leaves, measuring 3 to 5 feet across, have leaf stems armed with large teeth. The fruit is brownish black.

Care: This palm grows well in soil that is alkaline to slightly acidic and well drained. Occasionally potassium deficiency can develop, but regular feeding with a slow-release potassium fertilizer should prevent the problem. The plant grows at a moderate rate and has good salt and drought tolerance.

Recommended uses: The spiral leaf bases on the trunk of carnauba wax palm are as attractive as the crown, so plant this palm where you can appreciate both features.

Corypha umbraculifera
ko-REYE-fuh um-brak-yoo-LIF-er-uh
Talipot palm

- Size: 60–80'H×30–40'W
- Light: Full sun
- Water: Low to moderate
- Minimum temperature: 32°F
- Features: Single-trunk fan-leaf palm with small teeth on leaf stems

The most massive of all fan palms, talipot palm likely comes from India and Sri Lanka, although its exact origins are unclear. The trunk is 3 feet thick but appears even bigger because—except on tall trunks—the old leaf bases cover it. The bright green circular leaves are immense at 10 feet across. The leaves of younger plants tend to be larger than those of mature specimens. The leaf stems are armed with teeth along the margins. After 40 to 50 years the largest flower cluster in the plant kingdom emerges from the top of the palm. Going straight up and looking a bit like a Christmas tree, it produces tens of thousands of fruits one inch in diameter. After it finishes fruiting the palm dies.

Care: A slow grower to start, this palm grows quickly after a few years. It likes constant moisture but prefers well-drained soil that is either acidic or alkaline. It has no special nutrient needs, and its salt tolerance is fair.

Recommended uses: This enormous palm needs a large open area. When talipot's huge leaves fall they can devastate anything planted below. Instead consider mulching the area under the tree.

Talipot palm

Cryosophila stauracantha
kry-o-SAHF-ih-luh staw-ruh-KANTH-uh
Silver star palm

- Size: 20–25'H×8–10'W
- Light: Moderate to light shade
- Water: Moderate
- Minimum temperature: 30°F
- Features: Single-trunk fan-leaf palm with whitish leaf undersides

Silver star palm

Silver star palm is native to Belize, Guatemala, and Mexico. The light tan to gray trunk is often covered with long dull spines that are actually modified roots. The trunk diameter is 4 to 5 inches, and the spines are an inch or longer. The circular leaves, measuring 2 to 4 feet across, are deep green on top and silvery underneath. The fruit is white.

Care: This palm, which grows at a moderate rate, is not particular about soil as long as it drains well. It is not drought-tolerant, so water it regularly. It tolerates wet periods very well. Disease and pest problems are infrequent. The plant's salt tolerance is minimal.

Recommended uses: Silver star palm creates a beautiful secondary canopy under tall trees, and it also combines well with other tropical plants. Locate it where you can see both the top and bottom of the leaves and appreciate the color contrast.

Cyrtostachys renda
seer-toh-STAY-kiss REN-duh

Lipstick palm, Sealing wax palm

- **Size: 25–35'H×12–20'W**
- **Light: Moderate shade to full sun**
- **Water: Moderate to wet**
- **Minimum temperature: 35°F**
- **Features: Multitrunk feather-leaf palm with red crownshaft**

Lipstick palm

The most cherished form of this palm native to the swamps of Southeast Asia has a bright green trunk with conspicuous white rings 2 to 3 inches wide. The long crownshaft is the source of the plant's common name. It extends up through the leaf stem and is crimson, like a tube of lipstick. The 4- to 5-foot-long leaves are bright green on top and a bit lighter green underneath. The small fruit is shiny black.

Care: This beautiful palm is a moderately fast grower when its needs are met. It requires soil that is humusy and acidic. It prefers swampy, saturated soils and always needs a ready supply of water. Fertilize container-grown lipstick palms with high-nitrogen fertilizer to keep the leaves bright green. The plant tolerates full sun but looks best in some shade. It has no salt tolerance.

Recommended uses: Lipstick palm is exquisite no matter where you place it in the landscape. The plant does well in water features as long as the upper part of its soil is exposed to air. It also makes an attractive screen or hedge. You can grow it in a container.

Desmoncus polyacanthos
dez-MAHNK-us pah-lee-ay-KANTH-ohs

Surinam bramble palm

- **Size: 30–40'H×10–15'W**
- **Light: Heavy to moderate shade**
- **Water: Moderate**
- **Minimum temperature: 32°F**
- **Features: Multitrunk feather-leaf, vining palm with spines**

This vining rattan palm from northern South America forms a dense clump by pulling itself up through the canopy of larger trees. The trunks are less than an inch thick and are covered in thorny old leaf bases. The medium green leaves, to 6 feet long, end in an extension with backward hooks or spines that help it cling to surrounding objects. The trunks are used for making baskets and other woven products.

Care: The plant needs alkaline to slightly acidic soil that drains easily. It performs best with regular water and is not tolerant of drought or salt. No major disease or pest problems affect it.

Recommended uses: This palm is more of a curiosity than a specimen plant for a garden. Because it grows in the canopy of larger trees, you will catch only glimpses of the leaves as they poke through other greenery. Its thick growth can be part of an impenetrable privacy hedge. The leaf spines discourage attempts to pass through the barrier.

Surinam bramble palm

Dictyosperma album
dik-tee-o-SPURM-uh AL-bum

Princess palm, Hurricane palm

- **Size: 30–35'H×12–15'W**
- **Light: Full sun**
- **Water: Low to moderate**
- **Minimum temperature: 32°F**
- **Features: Single-trunk feather-leaf palm with crownshaft**

Princess palm

Princess palm comes from the Mascarene Islands in the Indian Ocean. The light tan or gray trunk, to 6 inches in diameter, is topped by a bulbous crownshaft that is whitish green, gray-green, or light green. The 8- to 12-foot-long leaves are deep green. The fruit is purplish black. The plant's other common name, hurricane palm, refers to its excellent tolerance to wind.

Care: Princess palm is slightly susceptible to lethal yellowing. The plant is not picky about soil other than it must drain freely. It thrives on regular water and fertilizer and has no major insect problems. Its salt tolerance is good, and its drought tolerance fair. It is a slow grower when young but eventually develops a moderate growth rate.

Recommended uses: This palm has long been overlooked for landscape use. It is ideal for open spaces, particularly when grown in a grouping of several plants at staggered heights. It works well in any size landscape and functions well as a street tree.

Drymophloeus litigiosus
Dry-MAHF-lee-us lih-tih-jee-O-sus
Beguine palm

- **Size: 10–12'H×5–7'W**
- **Light: Moderate to light shade**
- **Water: Moderate**
- **Minimum temperature: 32°F**
- **Features: Single-trunk feather-leaf palm with crownshaft**

Beguine palm

This palm, which comes from New Guinea, has a light tan trunk no more than 2 inches thick and often sits on a small mass of stilt roots (aboveground brace roots). The crownshaft is light green. Usually less than 4 feet long, the leaves are divided into regularly spaced wedge-shape leaflets of dark grassy green.
Care: Beguine palm prefers humusy acidic soil that drains well, but it tolerates slightly alkaline conditions well. It requires regular water and does not withstand drought. The plant grows at a moderate rate and has no special nutrient needs. It has no salt tolerance. Few disease or insect problems affect it.
Recommended uses: This palm's delicate appearance is appreciated best in an intimate spot where it can be seen up close. It looks best when planted with contrasting tropical foliage.

Dypsis baronii
DIP-sis bah-RO-nee-eye
Farihazo palm, Tongalo palm

- **Size: 15–20'H×10–12'W**
- **Light: Light shade**
- **Water: Moderate**
- **Minimum temperature: 32°F**
- **Features: Multitrunk feather-leaf palm with short crownshaft**

A native of Madagascar, farihazo palm has 3- to 4-inch-thick waxy blue-green trunks decorated with prominent rings left by the old leaves that fell off. The crownshaft is yellowish or light green. The leaves, to 6 feet long, are either medium or deep green. The fruit is bright yellow.
Care: Farihazo palm, which grows at a moderate pace, prefers well-drained acidic soil. It needs regular water and fertilizer. The plant dislikes drought and has little salt tolerance. It is not well adapted to the heat of South Florida summers.
Recommended uses: This palm is an ornamental addition to a landscape either as a stand-alone plant or at the edge of a planting bed, backed by other plants of contrasting color and shape. Locate it where you can enjoy it at close range.

Farihazo palm

Dypsis cabadae
DIP-sis kuh-BAH-dee
Cabada palm

- **Size: 30–35'H×10–15'W**
- **Light: Full sun**
- **Water: Low to moderate**
- **Minimum temperature: 32°F**
- **Features: Single- or multitrunk feather-leaf palm**

Cabada palm

Botanists first described cabada palm from cultivated plants found in the Cienfuegos Botanical Garden in Cuba. It has never been found in the wild, but Madagascar is assumed to be its home. The 3- to 5-inch-thick dark green trunk has white rings from old leaf scars. The medium to dark green leaves, 6 to 8 feet long, are beautifully arched. The single-trunk form tends to be larger in all aspects than the multitrunk form. The tiny fruit is crimson.
Care: Cabada palm prefers well-drained acidic soil but does quite well in alkaline soil as long as it, too, drains well. It is partial to regular water but tolerates short periods of drought. The plant has no special nutrient needs or major disease problems, and its tolerance to salt is slight.
Recommended uses: Both forms create a beautiful silhouette against a blank backdrop such as a wall, and they add elegance to a planting of foliage or flowering plants. Because the multitrunk form is a rather open clump, its use as a screening plant is limited unless you plant it with other dense vegetation.

Dypsis crinita
DIP-sis krih-NEET-uh

Vonitra palm

- **Size: 15–20'H×8–12'W**
- **Light: Moderate to light shade**
- **Water: Moderate to wet**
- **Minimum temperature: 32°F**
- **Features: Single- or multitrunk feather-leaf palm**

Vonitra palm

Found along rivers in Madagascar, vonitra palm grows as a single-trunk tree or forms sparse clumps. Trunks occasionally branch above ground. The 3- to 6-inch-thick trunk is covered in long hairy fibers from old leaf bases. The graceful leaves, measuring 6 to 8 feet long, emerge a translucent pinkish red and turn grassy green. The fruit is purplish black.

Care: Vonitra palm prefers humusy acidic soil, although it tolerates slight alkalinity. This palm, which grows at a moderate rate, does best when given copious amounts of water; it does not tolerate drought. Supplement regular fertilizer with iron to keep the plant greener. It has no salt tolerance.

Recommended uses: This palm is a natural for use around water features. Plant it in a spot where it gets some shade and where its full canopy of foliage and at least part of its hairy brown trunk are visible. The plant is also graceful when grouped.

Dypsis decaryi
DIP-sis deh-KAR-ee-eye

Triangle palm

- **Size: 25–30'H×12–15'W**
- **Light: Full sun**
- **Water: Drought tolerant**
- **Minimum temperature: 30°F**
- **Features: Single-trunk feather-leaf palm with leaves in three planes**

Triangle palm is endangered in its native Madagascar, but fortunately it has been widely cultivated so the species is in no danger of disappearing. Its common name comes from the leaves that radiate out in three distinct planes. The medium gray trunk ranges from 12 to 20 inches thick. The 8- to 10-foot-long leaves, which are V-shape and arch near their ends, can be deep green, gray-green, or blue-green. The fruit is nearly white. It is sometimes classified as *Neodypsis decaryi*.

Care: Growing at a moderate rate, this palm does well in acidic or alkaline soil that freely drains. It is quite drought-tolerant and has fair salt tolerance. The plant is quite susceptible to potassium deficiency, which causes dead leaf tips. It is slightly susceptible to lethal yellowing disease.

Recommended uses: Triangle palm will be a focal point no matter where you place it. The plant looks best as a specimen surrounded by lawn or a low groundcover. It is suited for use in formal gardens and also looks good as a container plant on a patio.

Triangle palm

Dypsis decipiens
DIP-sis deh-SIP-ee-enz

Manambe palm

- **Size: 30–35'H×12–15'W**
- **Light: Full sun**
- **Water: Low to moderate**
- **Minimum temperature: 28°F**
- **Features: Single- or multitrunk feather-leaf palm with crownshaft**

Manambe palm

This Madagascar native is either single trunked or forms a sparse clump. The 18- to 24-inch-thick medium gray trunk has evenly spaced rings from old leaf scars and is topped by a whitish green crownshaft. The deep green, arching leaves are 6 to 10 feet long. The fruit is yellowish.

Care: This slow-growing palm languishes or grows extremely slowly in the summer heat of South Florida but does well in California and Hawaii, where the nighttime lows are cooler. Manambe palm prefers well-drained acidic soil and regular water and fertilizer. It tolerates some drought and salt. The plant has no major pest problems.

Recommended uses: Manambe palm is impressive when planted by itself in an open area. You could plant a short groundcover underneath and around them, but any other vegetation would only detract from their grand presence.

Dypsis lanceolata
DIP-sis lan-see-o-LAHT-uh

Ivovowo palm

- **Size: 25–30'H×12–15'W**
- **Light: Full sun**
- **Water: Low to moderate**
- **Minimum temperature: 32°F**
- **Features: Multitrunk feather-leaf palm with short crownshaft**

Ivovowo palm

A relatively new introduction from Comoros, a group of islands in the Indian Ocean, this plant is becoming a highly prized landscape palm. It is similar to cabada palm but is even more attractive. The 3- to 4-inch-thick green trunks have prominent rings and are topped by a powdery silvery green crownshaft. The glossy deep green leaves gracefully arch to 8 feet long, and the leaflets narrow to a drip tip. The tiny fruit is bright red.
Care: Ivovowo palm will grow in either acidic or alkaline soil as long as it drains easily. It needs regular water and fertilizer. The plant grows at a moderate rate and tolerates short dry periods and some salt. Mealybugs occasionally attack the base of the crown.
Recommended uses: Use this attractive palm as a specimen or with other tropical foliage plants. It makes a superb silhouette set off against a white wall and is also effective as a screen.

Dypsis leptocheilos
DIP-sis lep-toh-KEYE-los

Redneck palm, Teddy bear palm

- **Size: 30–35'H×12–15'W**
- **Light: Full sun**
- **Water: Low to moderate**
- **Minimum temperature: 32°F**
- **Features: Single-trunk feather-leaf palm with short fuzzy crownshaft**

Native to Madagascar, this palm has a 6- to 8-inch-diameter trunk that is nearly whitish green in the newer part fading to greenish gray in the older portion. The common names refer to the short crownshaft, which has a ruddy color and is fuzzy like a teddy bear. The 8- to 10-foot-long leaves are deep glossy green.
Care: This moderately fast-growing palm needs well-drained acidic to slightly alkaline soil. It appreciates moisture and grows best when watered freely. The plant has no salt tolerance. It has no special nutrient needs and no major disease or insect problems.
Recommended uses: With its two-toned trunk and rusty red collar topped by a mass of glossy deep green leaves, this palm is spectacularly attractive by itself in an open area or planted with several other redneck palms of staggered heights.

Redneck palm

Dypsis lutescens
DIP-sis loo-TES-enz

Butterfly palm, Areca palm

- **Size: 25–30'H×15–20'W**
- **Light: Moderate shade to full sun**
- **Water: Low to moderate**
- **Minimum temperature: 32°F**
- **Features: Multitrunk feather-leaf palm**

Butterfly palm

This Madagascar native is heavily cultivated. Call it butterfly palm to avoid any misunderstanding; its other common name, areca palm, often confuses it with plants in the genus *Areca*. The 2- to 4-inch trunks are light waxy green in their newer sections and light olive green in their older parts. The 6- to 8-foot-long leaves, which arch gracefully (the palm's best attribute), vary from deep green to light yellowish green. The leaf stems are golden yellow. The fruit is greenish yellow to orange on nitrogen-deficient plants.
Care: Butterfly palm can take either acidic or alkaline soil but must have good drainage. The plant grows at a moderate pace and needs regular water and fertilizer. Its salt tolerance is fair. The species has few disease or insect problems, though spider mites may become a problem when it is grown indoors.
Recommended uses: Butterfly palm works well as a specimen in an open space or when massed as a screen. It is commonly grown indoors as a potted plant.

Dypsis madagascariensis
DIP-sis mad-uh-gas-kar-ee-EN-sis

Malagasy palm

- ■ **Size:** 30–35'H×15–20'W
- ■ **Light:** Full sun
- ■ **Water:** Low to moderate
- ■ **Minimum temperature:** 30°F
- ■ **Features:** Single- or multitrunk feather-leaf palm with crownshaft

Malagasy palm

This Madagascar native has 6- to 8-inch-thick trunks that are gray-green, especially in the younger portions, and prominently ringed with old leaf scars. The short crownshaft is powdery light green. The nicely arched dark green leaves grow to 10 feet long. The fruit is purplish.
Care: This palm needs soil that drains easily but can be either acidic or alkaline. It prefers regular water, although it tolerates short dry spells. The plant grows at a moderate rate and has no special nutrient needs. Its salt tolerance is minimal.
Recommended uses: A grouping of the single-trunk form is attractive with either lawn or a low groundcover planting around it. The multitrunk form is appealing as an isolated planting in an open area or incorporated into the background of a planting bed. They also can be used as a screen when partnered with other plants.

Dypsis pinnatifrons
DIP-sis pin-NAT-ih-frahnz

Madagascan palm

- ■ **Size:** 15–20'H×4–6'W
- ■ **Light:** Heavy to moderate shade
- ■ **Water:** Moderate
- ■ **Minimum temperature:** 32°F
- ■ **Features:** Solitary feather-leaf palm with short crownshaft

The trunk of this Madagascar native, measuring 2 to 4 inches in diameter, is greenish in its younger part and turns gray or brown as it ages. The crownshaft ranges from powdery green to pink. The dramatically curved 3- to 5-foot-long leaves are the plant's most attractive feature. The new foliage emerges burgundy to red and changes to glossy deep green. The oval leaflets are arranged in groups on the leaf stem and often end in a drip tip. The fruit is brown.
Care: Moderately fast-growing Madagascan palm needs acidic soil that drains well. It wants regular water and has no special fertilizer needs. The plant does best with constant humidity and warmth. It has no salt tolerance.
Recommended uses: This palm looks best with other tropical foliage plants but where its full crown of foliage can be viewed up close. It is also effective planted in groups.

Madagascan palm

Elaeis guineensis
el-EE-iss gihn-ee-EN-sis

African oil palm

- ■ **Size:** 50–60'H×20–25'W
- ■ **Light:** Full sun
- ■ **Water:** Low to moderate
- ■ **Minimum temperature:** 32°F
- ■ **Features:** Single-trunk feather-leaf palm with spiny leaf stems

African oil palm

A rain forest plant from West Africa, this palm is the primary source for commercial palm oil. In the tropics it is heavily cultivated in palm plantations where its fruit and seeds are processed for their oil. The trunk grows to 2 feet thick and is covered in old leaf bases except in its oldest part. The 15-foot-long leaves are dark green. The leaf stems are armed with large dull spines, which are actually modified leaflets. The black fruit is borne on bracts that grow among the leaf bases and thus are not easily seen.
Care: Moderately fast-growing African oil palm does well in acidic soil that is well drained. The plant prefers regular water and fertilizer applications. It tolerates short dry periods and has some salt tolerance.
Recommended uses: Often referred to as the poor man's Canary Island date palm (*Phoenix canariensis*), African oil palm has many of the same uses in the landscape. It is not quite as formal in appearance or as tidy, but it is magnificent in open spaces or along avenues. Other vegetation planted around it detracts from its overall appearance, so avoid using plants that will compete for attention.

Euterpe edulis
yoo-TURP-ee ED-yoo-lis
Assai palm

- **Size:** 30–35'H×12–15'W
- **Light:** Light shade to full sun
- **Water:** Moderate to wet
- **Minimum temperature:** 32°F
- **Features:** Single-trunk feather-leaf palm with crownshaft

Assai palm

Assai palm is a native of Brazil, Paraguay, and Argentina. Leaves, crownshaft, and upper trunk are all glossy emerald green. The trunk can be 6 inches thick with whitish rings prominent in its newer part. Leaves are up to 10 feet long and develop droopy leaflets. The edible fruits are purplish black when ripe. Assai palm is the source of palm heart that is harvested, canned, and distributed in jars on grocery store shelves. The tree dies once the palm heart is harvested, but it is easy to farm.

Care: Acidic soil that drains well and contains some organic matter is best for growing assai palm. Water it regularly; it is not drought-tolerant. Regular fertilization is sufficient to maintain robust growth. It is a fast-growing palm that has no salt tolerance.

Recommended uses: Assai palm is best when used in groupings to enhance its slender nature. It tolerates full sun when older, but until then, needs some protection from direct sun. Its best landscape asset is its overall deep green appearance.

Euterpe oleracea
yoo-TURP-ee o-leh-RAY-see-uh
Açai palm

- **Size:** 45–50'H×30–40'W
- **Light:** Light shade to full sun
- **Water:** Moderate to wet
- **Minimum temperature:** 32°F
- **Features:** Multitrunk feather-leaf palm with crownshaft

A native of South America, açai palm is a clump-former that occasionally grows as a solitary specimen. The 3- to 5-inch-wide trunks are deep green in their younger parts and light gray in their older parts. The crownshafts and leaves are also glossy deep green. Leaves are 6 to 10 feet long with pendent leaflets. Fruits turn purple when mature. They are the source of açai berry juice that can be found in health food stores. The heart of açai palm is also sometimes harvested, but it is less desirable than that of assai palm.

Care: Açai palm prefers copious amounts of water in an acidic soil. It does not tolerate drought so keep it well watered. This fast-growing palm has no special nutrient needs or serious insect or disease problems.

Recommended uses: With its pendent leaflets, açai palm is extremely graceful. It is excellent planted alone with no other plants nearby. Its willowy form looks natural near water features or used as a backdrop to other low-growing vegetation.

Açai palm

Gaussia maya
GOWS-ee-uh my-uh
Maya palm

- **Size:** 30–35'H×8–10'W
- **Light:** Light shade to full sun
- **Water:** Drought tolerant to low
- **Minimum temperature:** 30°F
- **Features:** Single-trunk feather-leaf palm with crimson fruit

Maya palm

Maya palm is native to Mexico, Belize, and Guatemala, where it grows primarily on limestone outcroppings. The light gray trunk is prominently ringed and seldom more than 6 inches wide; in time the trunk may develop a curve that looks lovely in the landscape. The medium green leaves are 4 to 6 feet long and arched. The fruit is crimson.

Care: Well-drained alkaline soil is most appropriate for maya palm, though it tolerates slightly acid conditions. This moderately fast-growing palm does not withstand wet conditions but is drought-tolerant. The plant performs well with regular light watering and regular feeding. It has some salt tolerance and no major disease or pest problems.

Recommended uses: Maya palm looks best used in a grouping of various heights. It's especially attractive when planted with small vegetation. It also works well as a canopy palm in small areas.

Geonoma interrupta
jee-o-NO-muh in-ter-UP-tuh

Chontilla palm

- **Size:** 12–15'H×5–8'W
- **Light:** Heavy shade
- **Water:** Moderate
- **Minimum temperature:** 32°F
- **Features:** Single- or multitrunk feather-leaf palm

Chontilla palm

Native to the Lesser Antilles, Central America, and northern South America, chontilla is a variable but easy-to-cultivate palm. The 2- to 4-inch-thick trunk is tan. The light to deep green leaflets that make up the 4- to 6-foot-long leaves vary in width and spacing.

Care: Growing at a moderate pace, chontilla palm does best in acidic to slightly alkaline soil that has some organic matter mixed in. The plant needs regular water and constant humidity. It is not tolerant of drought or salt, and it has no special nutrient needs. Occasionally spider mites can be a problem.

Recommended uses: The single-trunk form of chontilla palm is most commonly grown. It has a dainty appearance when small. The plant needs a sheltered intimate area so it can be viewed at close range.

Guihaia argyrata
gwee-HEYE-uh ar-jeye-RAH-tuh

Chinese needle palm

- **Size:** 5–7'H×5–7'W
- **Light:** Heavy to moderate shade
- **Water:** Drought tolerant to low
- **Minimum temperature:** 28°F
- **Features:** Multitrunk fan-leaf palm with needlelike fibers

A native of China and Vietnam, Chinese needle palm eventually develops short trunks covered in brown spiky fibers. The circular leaves, 2 to 3 feet across, are deep green on top and bronzy silver underneath. The small fruit is black when ripe.

Care: Very slow-growing Chinese needle palm prefers freely draining alkaline to neutral soil, although it tolerates some acidity. It appreciates light regular watering. The plant tolerates short dry spells and has a slight salt tolerance. It doesn't have any special nutrient needs or unusual pest problems.

Recommended uses: This palm is a treasure in the garden and its small stature allows for excellent eye-level viewing. Use it as a beautiful small specimen plant or scatter several within a planting area. Place other foliage plants far enough away so they do not compete with Chinese needle palm's form and charm.

Chinese needle palm

Heterospathe elata
het-er-o-SPAY-thee ee-LAHT-uh

Sagisi palm

- **Size:** 45–50'H×12–15'W
- **Light:** Full sun
- **Water:** Drought tolerant to low
- **Minimum temperature:** 32°F
- **Features:** Single-trunk feather-leaf palm with pinkish new leaves

Sagisi palm

Sagisi palm comes from the Philippines, Micronesia, and the Molucca Islands. When the plant is a seedling, the trunk pulls itself into the ground; when it emerges, the palm makes a sudden growth spurt, developing a light tan trunk 6 to 10 inches thick. The leaves, which grow 6 to 10 feet long, emerge light pinkish bronze but quickly turn glossy deep green. The drooping leaflets add a soft quality to the palm's overall appearance. The mature fruit is white.

Care: This palm isn't fussy about soil as long as it drains well. It needs water and fertilizer on a regular basis. The plant has some salt tolerance and isn't bothered by any major disease or insect problems. Its growth rate is moderate after the initial spurt.

Recommended uses: Use sagisi palm in an open area; either cluster it or plant it on its own. It is equally at home in a bed with other foliage plants. This palm softens harsh architectural lines of homes and walls when planted near them.

Howea belmoreana
how-ee-uh bel-mor-ee-AHN-uh

Sentry palm, Curly kentia palm

- **Size:** 25–30'H×8–10'W
- **Light:** Heavy to moderate shade
- **Water:** Drought tolerant to low
- **Minimum temperature:** 30°F
- **Features:** Single-trunk feather-leaf palm with arched leaves

Sentry palm

Similar in appearance to its cousin kentia palm, this native of Lord Howe Island off the coast of Australia differs mainly in its strongly arched leaves, which are deep green and 6 to 10 feet long. The younger portion of the 4- to 6-inch-thick trunk is dark green. The base of the trunk is somewhat swollen, and the leaf scars leave prominent rings. The fruit is red.

Care: Sentry palm's growth rate is quite slow. The plant does poorly in South Florida; it prefers cooler summer weather. It needs well-drained acidic soil and regular water and fertilizer. The plant has no salt tolerance. In California it tolerates full sun when taller but needs shade as a small plant.

Recommended uses: This palm makes a gorgeous container plant outdoors as well as in the house. In the landscape it is striking by itself—it creates a beautiful distinctive silhouette—or with other curly kentia palms and little else planted around them.

Howea forsteriana
how-ee-uh for-ster-ee-AHN-uh

Kentia palm, Sentry palm

- **Size:** 35–40'H×12–15'W
- **Light:** Heavy shade to full sun
- **Water:** Drought tolerant to low
- **Minimum temperature:** 30°F
- **Features:** Single-trunk feather-leaf palm with greenish trunk

Native to Lord Howe Island, kentia palm is a vision of grace and elegance. Its heavily ringed trunk is 4 to 6 inches thick and dark green in its younger portion. The 8- to 12-foot-long deep green leaves ascend with a gentle arch; each leaf has slightly droopy leaflets. The orangish red ripe fruit hangs from the plant in attractive elongated clusters.

Care: Slow-growing kentia palm prefers cool nights; it tolerates the full sun of California but needs shade in South Florida. This palm grows best in well-drained acidic to slightly alkaline soil. It prefers regular water but has some drought tolerance. The plant has no special fertilizer needs and is slightly susceptible to lethal yellowing. Its salt tolerance is low.

Recommended uses: Kentia palm is an outstanding container plant for indoor or outdoor use. When planted with several of its own kind in the landscape, it resembles coconut palm. If you plant it under the canopy of larger trees, use only small plants around its base.

Kentia palm

Hydriastele wendlandiana
heye-dree-uh-STEE-lee wend-land-dee-AHN-uh

Florence Falls palm

- **Size:** 30–35'H×8–10'W
- **Light:** Moderate to light shade
- **Water:** Moderate
- **Minimum temperature:** 32°F
- **Features:** Multitrunk feather-leaf palm with crownshaft

Florence Falls palm

Native to swampy areas in northern Australia, this palm is a clump former that occasionally is found as a single-trunk plant. The 3- to 6-inch-thick trunks are light gray, and the crownshaft light silvery green. The bright to dark green leaves, measuring 4 to 6 feet long, are made up of leaflets that vary in width and are arranged in clusters along the leaf stem. The fruit is red.

Care: This moderate grower prefers humusy soil that is acidic to slightly alkaline. It does not like to dry out and needs regular water. The plant has no special fertilizer needs and no major disease problems. Its tolerance to salt is slight.

Recommended uses: Florence Falls palm looks marvelous by itself in a relatively small area, its leaves creating a unique silhouette against the sky. Otherwise it should have contrasting foliage planted around it to bring its attractive good looks to life. As a screening plant it needs accompanying foliage to make an effective visual barrier.

Hyophorbe lagenicaulis
heye-o-FOR-bee lag-en-ih-KAWL-iss
Bottle palm

- **Size:** 12–15'H×6–8'W
- **Light:** Full sun
- **Water:** Drought tolerant
- **Minimum temperature:** 32°F
- **Features:** Single-trunk feather-leaf palm with crownshaft

Bottle palm

Native to the Mascarene Islands, this palm gets its common name from the shape of its trunk, which resembles a rounded bottle when the plant is young. As the palm ages the bottle shape elongates. At its thickest the light gray to tan trunk can measure 2 feet in diameter. The glossy dark green leaves, up to 6 feet long, arch elegantly. The crownshaft is a lighter green than the foliage. The fruit is dark green.

Care: Bottle palm maintains its best shape in full sun. It is not particular about soil as long as it drains well. The plant responds well to regular water but has some drought tolerance. It has good salt tolerance. Potassium deficiency is an occasional problem; treat it with fertilizer containing slow-release potassium.

Recommended uses: To fully appreciate the unusual shape of this palm, plant it in an open area surrounded only by lawn or a low-growing groundcover. A grouping of bottle palms is also extremely picturesque.

Hyophorbe verschaffeltii
heye-o-FOR-bee ver-shaf-ELT-ee-eye
Spindle palm

- **Size:** 20–25'H×8–10'W
- **Light:** Full sun
- **Water:** Drought tolerant
- **Minimum temperature:** 32°F
- **Features:** Single-trunk feather-leaf palm with crownshaft

The smooth columnar nearly white trunk of this native of the Mascarene Islands is 12 to 15 inches thick. The crownshaft is bluish green to olive green. The 5- to 6-foot-long bright green to olive green leaves arch near their ends. The fruit is black.

Care: Spindle palm, which grows at a moderate rate, does well in either acidic or alkaline soil that drains well. It tolerates drought but looks its best when given regular water and fertilizer. The plant develops a potassium deficiency at times; apply slow-release potassium regularly to prevent the problem or as a supplement to correct it. Spindle palm is slightly susceptible to lethal yellowing. Its salt tolerance is good.

Recommended uses: This palm is best suited to a wide, open area—perhaps in a lawn or a low groundcover—where its form can be appreciated. A grouping of spindle palms is sure to be a focal point in the landscape.

Spindle palm

Hyphaene thebaica
heye-FEE-nee thee-BAH-ih-kuh
Gingerbread palm

- **Size:** 35–40'H×30–40'W
- **Light:** Full sun
- **Water:** Drought tolerant
- **Minimum temperature:** 28°F
- **Features:** Multitrunk branched fan-leaf palm with teeth on leaf stems

Gingerbread palm

Originally from North Africa, gingerbread palm clumps slightly and branches freely above ground, at times creating a large canopy tree. The trunks are up to a foot thick and hold onto the old leaf bases except in their oldest parts. The 5- to 6-foot-long leaves are olive to grayish green. The bell-shape fruit is dark brown.

Care: Slow-growing gingerbread palm is very drought-resistant. The plant requires freely drained soil that is either acidic or alkaline. It has good salt tolerance. No specific nutrient needs or disease problems are associated with this palm.

Recommended uses: A large open space is ideal for this uniquely attractive palm. A group of these palms will stand out handsomely in a landscape—just be sure you have enough room to accommodate their eventual size.

Johannesteijsmannia altifrons
yo-hah-nes-tysh-MAHN-nee-uh AL-tih-frahnz
Joey palm

- **Size: 8–10'H×8–10'W**
- **Light: Heavy shade**
- **Water: Moderate to wet**
- **Minimum temperature: 35°F**
- **Features: Single-trunk palm with diamond-shape undivided leaves**

Joey palm

Spectacular is the best way to describe this native of Borneo, Malaysia, Thailand, and Sumatra. It forms no visible trunk; the crown of the palm appears to sit on the ground. The big diamond-shape leaves, to 10 feet long, are deep green with a distinct yellow stripe running along the middle of the leaf underside. The leaf and stems are armed with tiny teeth along their margins.

Care: Joey palm is particular about its growing conditions. It needs constant warmth and humidity as well as humusy acidic soil that is well drained. Never allow the soil to dry out. Regular fertilizer is sufficient for this slow grower. It has no salt tolerance.

Recommended uses: A magnificent palm like this demands an intimate spot where it can be seen at close range. Provide open space around it to fully appreciate the leaf shape and plant form.

Jubaea chilensis
joo-BEE-uh chil-EN-sis
Chilean wine palm

- **Size: 60–80'H×20–25'W**
- **Light: Full sun**
- **Water: Drought tolerant**
- **Minimum temperature: 28°F**
- **Features: Single-trunk feather-leaf palm with a massive smooth trunk**

Both the botanical and common name make it obvious that this palm comes from Chile, where it grows in the Andean foothills. The medium gray columnar trunk can be 6 feet in diameter. The dark olive green leaves are 8 to 12 feet long. The fruit is yellowish orange, and on occasion its seeds (which taste much like coconut) can be found in grocery stores.

Care: Chilean wine palm prefers acidic soil that drains well. It is drought-tolerant once established but prefers regular water, especially when young. This slow grower does well with regular fertilizer. No major disease or insect problems affect it. It prefers a Mediterranean climate and will not tolerate Florida summers. Its salt tolerance is fair.

Recommended uses: This massive palm needs a large landscape to maintain proper scale. It looks best in an open space with no other plants around it. If there is enough room, groupings of these giants are incredibly impressive. Avoid planting it in small gardens.

Chilean wine palm

Kentiopsis oliviformis
kent-ee-AHP-sis o-liv-ih-FOR-mis
Kentiopsis palm

- **Size: 45–60'H×10–12'W**
- **Light: Light shade to full sun**
- **Water: Moderate**
- **Minimum temperature: 30°F**
- **Features: Single-trunk feather-leaf palm with crownshaft**

Kentiopsis palm

This New Caledonia native has a 10- to 12-inch-thick trunk with a swollen base. In its younger part the trunk is green with prominent rings; the color changes to gray in the older portion. The bulging crownshaft is purplish green. The crown of 10- to 12-foot-long deep green leaves rising from the trunk makes this palm look like a giant feather duster.

Care: This plant, which grows at a moderate rate, succeeds in acidic or alkaline soil that drains well. It wants regular water and fertilizer. This palm does not tolerate drought and has only a slight salt tolerance. It has no special nutrient needs or unusual insect or disease problems.

Recommended uses: A splendid beauty like this is magnificent alone in an open space but is even better when several are planted in a group. It looks equally good planted with other tropical foliage plants beneath it as long as the feather duster effect is visible.

Kerriodoxa elegans
kair-ee-oh-DOX-uh EL-eh-ganz

Elegant palm

- Size: 8–10'H×10–12'W
- Light: Heavy to moderate shade
- Water: Moderate
- Minimum temperature: 30°F
- Features: Single-trunk fan-leaf palm with whitish silver leaf undersides

Elegant palm

Native to Thailand, where it grows as an understory species in wet forests, elegant palm eventually develops a trunk 6 to 8 inches in diameter. The rounded leaves grow to 6 feet across; the medium to dark green top surface contrasts sharply with the whitish silver underside. The mature fruit is yellowish white.

Care: Elegant palm does not tolerate dry conditions. It thrives on regular water in well-drained acidic to somewhat alkaline soil, preferably containing some organic matter. This slow-growing palm needs only regular fertilizer. It has little salt or drought tolerance. Diseases and insect pests do not affect the plant.

Recommended uses: A marvelous addition to the landscape, elegant palm becomes a focal point wherever it is planted. A single plant creates a splendid landscape effect. Place it in the middle of a planting bed with other contrasting tropical foliage to heighten its effect.

Laccospadix australasica
lak-ko-SPAY-dix aw-stral-AY-zih-kuh

Atherton palm

- Size: 10–15'H×8–10'W
- Light: Heavy shade
- Water: Moderate
- Minimum temperature: 30°F
- Features: Single- or multitrunk feather-leaf palm

This palm usually forms a clump but at times is single trunked. The clumping form has multiple trunks that are about 2 inches in diameter. In the single-trunk form they are double that thickness. The gracefully arching dark green leaves can reach 6 feet long; the new leaves often emerge a beautiful deep red. The fruit is bright red.

Care: Slow-growing Atherton palm prefers acidic soil that is well drained. It requires regular water. The plant is neither drought-tolerant nor salt-tolerant. It has no special nutrient needs or disease problems. Because Atherton palm grows at 2,500- to 4,500-foot elevations in its native Australia, it does best in areas with cool night temperatures.

Recommended uses: With its arching foliage and emergent red new growth, Atherton palm makes a nice accent. Both forms of Atherton palm are attractive in planting beds with other flowering or foliage plants. The single-trunk form in particular looks good in a grouping.

Atherton palm

Latania loddigesii
la-TAN-ee-uh lo-dih-GEH-zee-eye

Blue latan palm

- Size: 20–25'H×10–15'W
- Light: Full sun
- Water: Drought tolerant
- Minimum temperature: 32°F
- Features: Single-trunk fan-leaf palm with silvery blue leaves

Blue latan palm

Blue latan palm is a native of the Mascarene Islands. Its light gray trunk is bulbous at the base and about 10 inches thick through the rest of the trunk. The leaves, which grow 4 to 5 feet wide, are green with red margins when young but become silvery blue as the palm ages. Separate male and female plants are needed to produce fruit, which is brown and contains one to three seeds.

Care: Slow-growing blue latan is not fussy about soil as long as it is well drained. The plant is somewhat drought-tolerant but likes regular water. It has no special nutrient needs or disease problems other than a slight susceptibility to lethal yellowing disease. Its salt tolerance is quite good.

Recommended uses: This palm stands out in the landscape, so use it as a focal point. It works well as a stand-alone feature or with other contrasting plants at its base. A grouping of several blue latan palms at staggered heights is striking.

Licuala grandis
lih-KWAHL-uh GRAND-iss

Ruffled fan palm

- **Size:** 10–12'H×6–8'W
- **Light:** Moderate to light shade
- **Water:** Moderate
- **Minimum temperature:** 32°F
- **Features:** Single-trunk fan-leaf palm with corrugated undivided leaves

Ruffled fan palm

Originally from Vanuatu and the Solomon Islands, ruffled fan palm has a gray to tan trunk 2 to 3 inches in diameter. The grassy to deep green undivided leaves, measuring 2 to 3 feet wide, are pleated. The leaf stems have small teeth along the margins. The ripe fruit is red.
Care: Slow-growing ruffled fan palm prefers well-drained acidic soil but tolerates somewhat alkaline soil. It does not withstand drought; water it regularly. To keep the foliage deep green, supplement its regular feeding with iron. The plant has no particular pest or disease problems and no salt tolerance. As a houseplant, ruffled fan palm needs bright light and high humidity.
Recommended uses: With a low groundcover planted around it, this charming palm becomes a focal point. It is also an exquisite container plant for the patio or in a bright location indoors.

Licuala lauterbachii
lih-KWAHL-uh lau-ter-BAHK-ee-eye

Bougainville palm

- **Size:** 10–12'H×6–8'W
- **Light:** Moderate shade
- **Water:** Moderate
- **Minimum temperature:** 32°F
- **Features:** Single-trunk fan-leaf palm with deeply divided leaves

Native to New Guinea, this palm tends to grow smaller in cultivation than in its native setting. It has a grayish trunk 2 to 3 inches thick. The glossy deep green circular leaves, measuring 3 to 4 feet across, are evenly segmented with deep divisions. The leaf stems are armed with small teeth. The fruit is orangish red when ripe.
Care: This slow-growing palm needs acidic soil that is well drained and has some organic matter mixed in. The plant appreciates regular water and fertilizer. Its tolerance for salt is very low. It has no special nutrient needs and few disease problems.
Recommended uses: The plant looks superb in an intimate part of the garden where it can be viewed up close. It looks equally attractive as a specimen or grouped. Do not obscure the leaf crown with other plants. This palm also makes an excellent container plant.

Bougainville palm

Licuala mattanensis 'Mapu'
lih-KWAHL-uh mat-uh-NEN-sis mah-POO

Mapu palm

- **Size:** 1–2'H×1–2'W
- **Light:** Heavy shade
- **Water:** Moderate
- **Minimum temperature:** 35°F
- **Features:** Single-trunk fan-leaf palm with mottled leaves

Mapu palm

One of the smallest of all palms, this variety developed from a species native to Borneo. It is a groundcover plant that develops a very short trunk after many years. The mature leaves almost always are split into 11 segments with the center segment much narrower than the rest. The leaf color is glossy deep green with light yellow mottling throughout.
Care: Mapu palm is demanding when it comes to care. The plant needs humusy acidic soil that stays moist but drains well, high humidity and regular watering with never a dry day, and regular fertilizer. It won't tolerate freezing temperatures or exposure to salt. If you can provide suitable growing conditions for this palm, you will be richly rewarded with one of the most beautiful palms available.
Recommended uses: Plant mapu palm where you can enjoy it at close range. A mass planting makes a gorgeous groundcover.

Licuala peltata sumawongii
lih-KWAHL-uh pel-TAHT-uh soo-muh-WONG-ee-eye

Elegant licuala

- **Size:** 12–15'H×10–12'W
- **Light:** Moderate to light shade
- **Water:** Moderate
- **Minimum temperature:** 30°F
- **Features:** Single-trunk fan-leaf palm with undivided leaves

Elegant licuala

A native of Thailand and Malaysia, elegant licuala has a tan trunk about 3 inches across. The undivided rounded leaves, measuring 5 to 6 feet across, are glossy bright green to deep green depending on the amount of shade. (Deeper green develops in more intense shade.) The leaf stem is armed with spines along its margins. The fruit is bright red.
Care: Like others in the genus, this palm prefers humusy acidic soil that drains well but stays moist. It does not tolerate drought or salt. The plant, which grows at a slow to moderate rate, requires regular water and fertilizer applications. Extra iron is helpful in maintaining good color. The palm needs protection from wind, which can tatter the leaves.
Recommended uses: This elegant palm creates a statement when it is planted in the right location. Use it as a focal point under a tree canopy. Several planted under a large feather-leafed palm make a stunning combination.

Licuala ramsayi
lih-KWAHL-uh RAM-zay-eye

Australian licuala

- **Size:** 20–25'H×8–10'W
- **Light:** Moderate shade
- **Water:** Moderate
- **Minimum temperature:** 32°F
- **Features:** Single-trunk fan-leaf palm with circular leaves

The swamps in Queensland, Australia, where this palm grows twice as tall as in gardens, are an incredible sight. Atop the 3- to 6-inch-thick light gray trunk are dark green leaves 5 to 6 feet across that look like huge pinwheels. The mature fruit is red.
Care: Slow-growing Australian licuala needs humusy acidic soil that drains well. A constant supply of moisture is essential for robust growth. Regular fertilizer applications with occasional iron supplements maintains good color. The plant has no salt tolerance. It isn't bothered by any serious insect or disease problems.
Recommended uses: This palm makes an excellent focal point. Plant it where it can show off its magnificent features. It is just as attractive planted in a cluster. When it becomes tall enough for you to stand under and look up at the leaves, you'll find that it creates a wonderful silhouette against the sky.

Australian licuala

Licuala spinosa
lih-KWAHL-uh spin-O-suh

Spiny licuala

- **Size:** 20–25'H×15–20'W
- **Light:** Moderate shade to full sun
- **Water:** Moderate
- **Minimum temperature:** 28°F
- **Features:** Multitrunk fan-leaf palm with teeth on leaf stems

Spiny licuala; ripe fruits (inset)

A native of Southeast Asia, spiny licuala gets its common name from the rather large spines along both margins of the leaf stems. The trunks of this dense clumper are 2 to 3 inches thick and generally covered in old leaf bases. The leaves, which can measure over 2 feet across, are circular and deeply divided into even segments, and the color ranges from light green in full sun to deep green in moderate shade. The mature fruit is red.
Care: Spiny licuala is a water lover. It does not appreciate dry conditions but tolerates wet periods well. The plant thrives in humusy, fairly well-drained soil. Regular fertilizer applications with occasional extra iron will keep it healthy. The most cold-hardy species in the genus, this palm grows at a moderate rate and has some salt tolerance.
Recommended uses: Spiny licuala looks good planted alone surrounded by open space. It's also at home around water features and can be a good screening plant.

Livistona australis
liv-ih-STON-uh aw-STRAL-iss
Australian cabbage palm

- **Size:** 45–50'H×12–15'W
- **Light:** Full sun
- **Water:** Drought tolerant to low
- **Minimum temperature:** 25°F
- **Features:** Single-trunk fan-leaf palm with teeth on leaf stems

Australian cabbage palm

From its species name you can correctly guess that this palm comes from Australia. The 10- to 12-inch-thick trunk is brown to gray. The deep green leaves grow to 5 feet across; the last 12 to 18 inches of the leaf segments droop, giving the palm a willowy appearance. The leaf stems are armed with teeth along their margins. The fruit is black.
Care: Australian cabbage palm, which grows at a moderate pace, is easy to care for. It is not particular about soil as long as it drains well. Regular water and fertilizer will keep it growing robustly. The plant has a slight tolerance for drought and salt.
Recommended uses: This handsome willowy palm is a standout when planted alone or in a group. It creates a beautiful tropical silhouette as a canopy palm and looks good with a short groundcover planted beneath it.

Livistona chinensis
liv-ih-STON-uh chih-NEN-sis
Chinese fan palm

- **Size:** 30–40'H×15–18'W
- **Light:** Full sun
- **Water:** Drought tolerant to low
- **Minimum temperature:** 25°F
- **Features:** Single-trunk fan-leaf palm with teeth on leaf stems

Widely cultivated throughout the world, Chinese fan palm is native to Taiwan and southern Japan. The trunk, about a foot in diameter, is gray. The leaves, to 4 feet across, are glossy bright green when the palm is young and olive green in mature plants. The leaf stem margins are armed with teeth that often disappear in older specimens. The fruit is turquoise blue at maturity.
Care: This slow to moderate grower is not fussy about soil as long as it drains well. It thrives on regular water and fertilizer. The plant tolerates dry periods and has fair salt tolerance. It has a slight susceptibility to lethal yellowing disease.
Recommended uses: One reason that Chinese fan palm is commonly grown is that it's versatile. A single specimen or several look equally good. It is attractive planted in the open or with other plants around it. This is an ideal palm to use in a formal garden or informal tropical setting.

Chinese fan palm

Livistona decora
liv-ih-STON-uh deh-KOR-uh
Ribbon fan palm

- **Size:** 40–50'H×15–20'W
- **Light:** Full sun
- **Water:** Drought tolerant to low
- **Minimum temperature:** 25°F
- **Features:** Single-trunk fan-leaf palm with weeping leaves

Ribbon fan palm

This native of Australia has a light brown to light gray trunk 10 to 12 inches thick. The 6-foot-long deep olive green leaves are deeply divided, causing the leaf segments to droop for about half their length and creating a delightful weeping effect. The leaf stems have nasty teeth along their margins. The ripe fruit is black.
Care: Ribbon fan palm handles acidic or alkaline soil equally well as long as it is well drained. The plant is a moderately fast grower, but if given copious amounts of water it grows much faster. It does well with regular fertilizer. It is not particularly drought tolerant but does have fair salt tolerance and few disease problems.
Recommended uses: The relaxed, weeping effect of ribbon fan palm's leaves give it a more informal appearance than a formal look. It works well standing alone or grouped. It also looks good surrounded by other lush tropical plants.

Livistona rotundifolia
liv-ih-STON-uh ro-tund-ih-FO-lee-uh
Footstool palm

- **Size: 40–50'H×12–15'W**
- **Light: Full sun**
- **Water: Drought tolerant to low**
- **Minimum temperature: 30°F**
- **Features: Single-trunk fan-leaf palm with glossy deep green leaves**

Footstool palm

Footstool palm is native to parts of Southeast Asia. The trunk, about 12 inches thick, is a beautiful waxy brown accented with regularly spaced rings where the old leaf bases fell off. The 5- to 6-foot-wide shallowly divided circular leaves are glossy bright or dark green. The fruit is scarlet, making the footstool palm extremely ornamental and colorful during its fruiting period.
Care: This moderate grower needs well-drained soil, but it tolerates either acidic or alkaline conditions. This plant requires regular water and fertilizer for robust growth. Its salt tolerance is fair. No major disease or nutrient problems affect it.
Recommended uses: Surround this palm with other foliage and flowering plants in a tropical setting. Choose a site where you can see the upper part of the trunk, leafy crown, and fruit. A single footstool palm silhouetted against the sky is delightful, and a grouping is even more picturesque.

Livistona saribus
liv-ih-STON-uh SAR-ih-bus
Taraw palm

- **Size: 35–45'H×15–18'W**
- **Light: Full sun**
- **Water: Drought tolerant to low**
- **Minimum temperature: 25–30°F**
- **Features: Single-trunk fan-leaf palm with large teeth on leaf stems**

From Southeast Asia taraw palm has a 10- to 14-inch-thick trunk that is gray in its older portion. As a young tree, taraw palm has leaves that are stiff, round, and divided into regular segments—creating a beautiful form that makes the plant look more like a licuala. Once it grows tall enough to reach full sun, it develops circular deep green leaves that measure 4 to 5 feet across, and the leaf stems are armed with vicious large teeth. One form of this species has green leaf bases, and the other red leaf bases. The green form appears to be several degrees hardier (to 25°F) than the red form (to 30°F). The mature fruit is purplish.
Care: This slow to moderate grower does well in either acidic or alkaline soil that drains well. The plant appreciates regular watering and fertilizer. It tolerates little salt. Although it is drought tolerant it also withstands short wet periods.
Recommended uses: As a stand-alone palm in the open or combined with other plants, taraw palm is a worthwhile addition to the landscape.

Taraw palm and trunk (inset)

Lodoicea maldivica
lo-DOY-see-uh mal-DIV-ih-kuh
Coco de mer

- **Size: 45–50'H×20–25'W**
- **Light: Light shade to full sun**
- **Water: Moderate**
- **Minimum temperature: 32°F**
- **Features: Single-trunk fan-leaf palm with unique large fruit and seed**

Coco de mer

This native of the Seychelle Islands is not only beautiful but also has the distinction of having the largest seed in the plant kingdom—a single one weighs up to 50 pounds. The gray trunk, which is slow to develop, has a diameter of 16 to 20 inches. The medium to dark green leaves can reach 18 feet long. After taking five to seven years to mature, the fruit turns black.
Care: Coco de mer palm is seldom cultivated outside the Seychelles. It is extremely slow growing and needs deep, well-drained soil. Warm weather and regular watering and fertilization are essential for good growth. The plant is not drought or salt tolerant. Protect the leaves from wind, which can tatter them.
Recommended uses: If you are fortunate enough to locate one of these palms, place it in a protected area under light shade. It looks incredible whether planted alone or with other plants. The large leaves will be the main focus of the plant.

Lytocaryum weddellianum
ly-to-KAR-ee-um wed-el-ee-AHN-um

Baby coconut palm

- **Size: 6–8'H×4–6'W**
- **Light: Heavy to moderate shade**
- **Water: Moderate**
- **Minimum temperature: 30°F**
- **Features: Single-trunk feather-leaf palm with deep green leaves**

Baby coconut palm

Native to the rain forest of coastal southeastern Brazil, this palm gets its common name from its resemblance to a miniature coconut palm. The 2- to 3-inch-thick trunk is covered in old leaf bases. The leaves, as long as 5 feet in deep shade, are deep emerald green on top and silvery gray beneath. The ripe bluish green fruit splits open to reveal a single brown seed.

Care: Moderately fast-growing baby coconut palm needs humusy acidic soil that drains well. The plant performs best with regular water and fertilizer. It does not tolerate sun, drought, or salt very well.

Recommended uses: Baby coconut palm is best used as an understory plant. It has a delicate appearance that is quite charming when planted in an intimate part of the garden with other foliage around it. This palm has long been used indoors in Europe, and it also does well in a container in a shady spot on the patio.

Marojejya darianii
mar-o-JEH-jee-uh dar-ee-AHN-ee-eye

Ravimbe palm

- **Size: 15–20'H×15–20'W**
- **Light: Moderate shade**
- **Water: Moderate**
- **Minimum temperature: 32°F**
- **Features: Single-trunk feather-leaf palm with huge undivided leaves**

The spectacular ravimbe palm is a native of Madagascar, where few of the plants remain in their native habitat. After many years this palm develops a trunk that can be a foot thick. The medium green undivided leaves can reach as much as 15 feet long and 4 feet wide.

Care: A slow to moderate grower, this palm requires soil that is acidic, fast draining, and has organic matter mixed in. It needs supplemental iron along with regular fertilizer. Regular water is important because the palm should never be allowed to dry out. The plant has no salt tolerance, and needs wind protection to prevent its immense leaves from tattering.

Recommended uses: Ravimbe palm looks best with no other competing plants around it, though it needs a high canopy above it to protect it from the sun. Avoid using this palm in groups; it is most effective on its own.

Ravimbe palm

Metroxylon sagu
meh-TRAHX-ih-lahn SAH-goo

Sago palm

- **Size: 40–60'H×20–30'W**
- **Light: Light shade to full sun**
- **Water: Wet**
- **Minimum temperature: 35°F**
- **Features: Multitrunk feather-leaf palm with sharp spines**

Sago palm

This palm has been cultivated for so long that its exact origin is unknown, though New Guinea is considered a likely candidate. The trunk, which can be 2 feet thick, is covered in its newer portion with old leaf bases bearing needlelike spines. These spines extend up through the leaf stem and midrib. The 15- to 20-foot leaves are medium to dark green, though newly emerging leaves may be pinkish. An immense flower cluster develops at the top of the palm. After it blooms and fruits, the stem dies. In some regions indigenous people harvest starch from the pith of the trunk just before the tree flowers; they use the starch as a food staple.

Care: Sago palm prefers acidic soil that remains on the wet side. It does not tolerate drought or salt. Regular fertilizer is sufficient for this fast grower.

Recommended uses: The plant looks especially at home around water features, but don't crowd it—this palm needs a large space in which to grow. It is especially attractive alone in an open area with no other plants around it.

Metroxylon salomonense
meh-TRAHX-ih-lahn sal-o-mo-NEN-see
Ivory nut palm

- **Size: 50–70'H×25–30'W**
- **Light: Full sun**
- **Water: Wet**
- **Minimum temperature: 35°F**
- **Features: Single-trunk feather-leaf palm with sharp spines**

Ivory nut palm

This immense palm comes from New Guinea, Vanuatu, and the Solomon Islands. The gray to brown trunk can be 4 feet in diameter. Deep green leaves to 30 feet long ascend and then arch near their ends, giving the palm the appearance of a giant shuttlecock. The leaf bases, leaf stems, and midribs are covered in needlelike spines. This palm sends out an immense flower cluster from its top, then produces thousands of fruits the size of tennis balls. After the plant has finished fruiting it dies.

Care: Ivory nut palm needs copious amounts of water regularly; it does not tolerate dry spells. Acidic soil that contains some organic matter is best for this fast grower. Regular fertilizer fulfills the plant's nutrient needs. It has no tolerance for salt.

Recommended uses: This handsome huge palm is best appreciated from a distance where its overall form can be seen. It is not suitable for a small space and should not be surrounded by other plants. Its silhouette is especially pleasing when it is in flower.

Nannorrhops ritcheana
NAN-o-rahps rich-ee-AHN-uh
Mazari palm

- **Size: 12–15'×12–15'W**
- **Light: Full sun**
- **Water: Drought tolerant to low**
- **Minimum temperature: 22–28°F**
- **Features: Multitrunk fan-leaf palm with green or bluish leaves**

Native to Afghanistan and Pakistan, mazari palm grows in dry mountainous areas by water sources. Some forms are much cold hardier than others. The trunks generally remain belowground but occasionally emerge to heights of 10 feet or more. The 2- to 3-foot-wide triangular leaves are olive green, greenish gray, or silvery blue. After a stem flowers it produces orangish brown fruit, then dies, but other stems in the clump continue to grow.

Care: Mazari palm grows slowly, especially in hot, humid climates. The plant is not particular about soil as long as it drains well; it does not tolerate wet conditions. Although it thrives on regular water, it is quite drought tolerant. The plant has good salt tolerance and no special nutrient needs. It is slightly susceptible to lethal yellowing.

Recommended uses: This palm looks good alone in an open space or with a backdrop of other plants. The silvery blue form is particularly attractive.

Mazari palm

Neoveitchia storckii
nee-o-VEECH-ee-uh STORK-ee-eye
Unleito palm

- **Size: 35–40'H×15–20'W**
- **Light: Light shade to full sun**
- **Water: Moderate**
- **Minimum temperature: 32°F**
- **Features: Single-trunk feather-leaf palm with purplish crownshaft**

Unleito palm

Native to Fiji this palm has a light tan trunk with a swollen base that is 10 to 12 inches thick. The short crownshaft is purplish black but turns green near the leaf stem. The graceful leaves, growing 8 to 12 feet long, are glossy deep green. The fruit is orange.

Care: This moderately fast-growing palm tolerates only brief cold snaps down to freezing. It succeeds in well-drained acidic or alkaline soil containing some organic material. The plant thrives on regular water and fertilizer. It has only slight tolerance for salt. It has no major insect or disease problems. It performs better with some shade when young.

Recommended uses: At home in a lush tropical setting with other plants, this palm is also a standout as a specimen.

Normanbya normanbyi
nor-MAN-bee-uh nor-MAN-bee-eye
Black palm

- **Size:** 35–40'H×8–12'W
- **Light:** Light shade to full sun
- **Water:** Moderate
- **Minimum temperature:** 30°F
- **Features:** Single-trunk feather-leaf palm with crownshaft

Black palm

This native of Australia looks much like foxtail palm, but the wood from the 6-inch-thick tannish trunk of this species is so hard that it is used in construction. The silvery green crownshaft bulges slightly. Very feathery 6- to 8-foot-long leaves are dark green on top and silvery green beneath. The ripe fruit is deep pink.

Care: Black palm needs well-drained acidic soil with some organic matter mixed in. Regular water is a must because the plant does not tolerate dry conditions well. This moderately fast grower needs only regular fertilizer and has no major disease or insect problems. Its salt tolerance is low. Older plants can tolerate full sun, but younger ones should be placed under a tall canopy for light shade.

Recommended uses: Try placing three to five black palms of staggered heights in an irregular pattern to achieve an especially beautiful effect.

Nypa fruticans
NEEP-uh FROOT-ih-kanz
Mangrove palm

- **Size:** 15–20'H×12–15'W
- **Light:** Light shade to full sun
- **Water:** Aquatic
- **Minimum temperature:** 35°F
- **Features:** Single-trunk feather-leaf palm that grows at water's edge

Mangrove palm is widespread throughout the Asian and Pacific tropics, where it usually grows along rivers just before they empty into the ocean. It has a prostrate branching trunk, which gives the appearance of a clumping palm. Roots form along the trunk as it travels sideways. The stems that branch upward are covered in old leaf bases and are 8 to 10 inches thick. The ascending leaves, to 20 feet long, range from yellow green to deep green from tree to tree. The chocolate brown fruit is arranged in a clublike bract. Because the fruit floats, currents carry it to an open spot of land where it can germinate.

Care: This palm gets its common name from its association with mangroves, which grow along coastal areas. Mangrove palm has excellent salt tolerance. It generally grows on the banks of brackish water, where it is partially submerged during high tides. The plant must have constant moisture. It rarely develops nutrient deficiencies.

Recommended uses: Place this palm only on the banks of a stream or pond containing brackish water.

Mangrove palm

Orania palindan
o-RAN-ee-uh PAL-in-dahn
Orania palm

- **Size:** 25–30'H×12–15'W
- **Light:** Full sun
- **Water:** Moderate
- **Minimum temperature:** 32°F
- **Features:** Single-trunk feather-leaf palm with drooping leaves

Orania palm

A native of the Philippines, this palm has a relatively smooth grayish trunk 10 to 12 inches thick. The deep green leaves to 8 feet long are held rather stiffly upright but have pendulous leaflets. The fruit is yellowish green. Members of this genus are the only poisonous palms. Avoid ingesting the palm heart, fruit, or seeds.

Care: This moderate grower is the most widely cultivated species in the genus because it is the most cold-tolerant. It grows well in either acidic or alkaline well-drained soil. It needs regular water and fertilizer applications to maintain good growth. Its salt tolerance is slight. Nutrient deficiencies are rare, and major pest problems are nonexistent.

Recommended uses: As a specimen or in a grouping, this palm is gorgeous. It also looks great against a backdrop of contrasting foliage or with a low groundcover planted underneath it.

Oraniopsis appendiculata
o-ran-ee-AHP-sis ap-pen-dik-yoo-LAHT-uh

Bronze palm

- **Size: 20–25'H×12–15'W**
- **Light: Moderate shade to full sun**
- **Water: Moderate**
- **Minimum temperature: 28°F**
- **Features: Single-trunk feather-leaf palm with silver leaf undersides**

Bronze palm

In its native habitat in Queensland, Australia, this palm can reach 60 feet or taller, but such specimens are extremely old. The gray trunk grows 10 to 12 inches in diameter. The leaves are deep green on top and light silver underneath. They are held stiffly upright and bear stiff leaflets in a single plane. The spherical fruit is orange.

Care: This is one of the slowest growing of all palms, requiring up to 30 years to develop a trunk. The plant prefers cool nights. It does best in well-drained acidic to slightly alkaline soil and likes regular water and fertilizer. Pests and nutrient deficiencies are rare. The plant's salt tolerance is minimal. It needs some shade when it's young; after many years it will tolerate full sun.

Recommended uses: An extremely ornamental palm like this is a standout in any garden whether planted by itself or in a group.

Parajubaea coccoides
par-uh-joo-BEE-uh kok-OI-deez

Quito coconut palm

- **Size: 40–50'H×15–18'W**
- **Light: Light shade to full sun**
- **Water: Drought tolerant to low**
- **Minimum temperature: 28°F**
- **Features: Single-trunk feather-leaf palm with arching leaves**

Quito coconut palm is known only in cultivation, and some experts think that it may be a cultivar of *P. torallyi*. It probably originated in the mountains of South America. Except in its oldest section the 18-inch-thick trunk is covered in hairy old leaf bases. The deep green arching leaves are 10 to 12 feet long. The fruit stems grow upright and bear brownish black fruits.

Care: This slow to moderate grower does not tolerate humid heat but does well in climates with cooler nights. It thrives in well-drained acidic to slightly alkaline soil. Regular water and fertilizer are best for good health. The plant has some drought tolerance and little salt tolerance. No major pest or disease problems affect it.

Recommended uses: This palm is impressive by itself but even more appealing when several are grouped. A low groundcover or small shrubs planted around the base add to its beauty.

Quito coconut palm

Pelagodoxa henryana
pel-uh-go-DAHX-uh hen-ree-AHN-uh

Yahanna palm

- **Size: 20–25'H×10–12'W**
- **Light: Light shade to full sun**
- **Water: Moderate**
- **Minimum temperature: 35°F**
- **Features: Single-trunk feather-leaf palm with undivided leaves**

Yahanna palm

A native of the Marquesas Islands in the Pacific Ocean, yahanna palm is unusual. Its most attractive feature is undivided leaves growing 6 to 7 feet long. Each leaf is deep dark green on top and silvery underneath. The gray trunk grows to 6 inches thick. The fruit, covered with warty bumps, is variable in size and tannish brown when mature.

Care: Wind shreds yahanna palm leaves, so growing the plant in a protected spot is important. A moderately fast grower, this palm thrives in well-drained acidic to slightly alkaline soil. It requires regular water and fertilizer. The plant is not drought-tolerant and only slightly salt-tolerant. It has no major insect or disease problems.

Recommended uses: Prominently display eyecatching yahanna palm. It doesn't need any companion plants, which will only distract from its good looks. Even though this palm tolerates full sun well, many people locate it under a canopy to protect it from wind.

Phoenix canariensis
FEE-nix kuh-nair-ee-EN-sis

Canary Island date palm

- **Size:** 50–70'H×25–30'W
- **Light:** Full sun
- **Water:** Drought tolerant
- **Minimum temperature:** 25°F
- **Features:** Single-trunk feather-leaf palm with spines on leaf stems

Canary Island date palm

As its name reveals, this palm comes from the Canary Islands. The massive brown trunk is 2 to 3 feet in diameter. The younger part is covered in old leaf bases while the older section exhibits a beautiful pattern of old leaf scars. The leaf stems are armed with large spines. The entire crown of 10- to 15-foot-long deep green leaves is spherical, giving the palm a lollipop look. The fruit is orange.

Care: Relatively slow-growing Canary Island date palm is not particular about soil as long as it drains freely. The plant is extremely drought-tolerant but responds well to light watering and regular feeding. It often develops a magnesium deficiency. It is highly susceptible to fusarium wilt and somewhat susceptible to lethal yellowing. Its salt tolerance is good.

Recommended uses: Canary Island date palm is the epitome of nobility. It has no equal in the formal garden and is superb for framing a multistory house. It also makes an excellent street tree.

Phoenix dactylifera
FEE-nix dak-tih-LIF-er-uh

Date palm

- **Size:** 50–60'H×20–25'W
- **Light:** Full sun
- **Water:** Drought tolerant
- **Minimum temperature:** 25°F
- **Features:** Multitrunk feather-leaf palm with bluish leaves

Date palm is the source of the date fruit found worldwide in grocery stores. Many cultivars are available. The exact origin of the palm is unknown but is likely somewhere in the Middle East or Africa. Although it is a clumping palm, in cultivation suckers are usually removed to create a single-trunk tree that occasionally branches. The silvery blue leaves are 10 to 15 feet long and armed with long spines along the leaf stems. The fruit ranges from golden yellow to red.

Care: This palm flourishes in well-drained acidic or alkaline soil. It is drought-tolerant but likes light regular watering and regular feeding. Its salt tolerance is good. Date palm is sometimes subject to a potassium deficiency. It is slightly susceptible to lethal yellowing and fusarium wilt. Insect pests are seldom a problem.

Recommended uses: Stately date palm is superb in a formal garden. It frames a multistory house beautifully. It needs no other plants around it but looks good when underplanted with shrubs. A street planting of date palms is a magnificent sight.

Date palm

Phoenix reclinata
FEE-nix rek-lih-NAH-tuh

Senegal date palm

- **Size:** 40–50'H×25–40'W
- **Light:** Full sun
- **Water:** Drought tolerant to low
- **Minimum temperature:** 28°F
- **Features:** Multitrunk feather-leaf palm with spines on leaf stems

Senegal date palm

Senegal date palm is native to tropical Africa, where it grows along the banks of streams. The 4- to 6-inch-thick trunks are covered in old leaf bases and fibers. The glossy green leaves are 10 to 12 feet long, and the leaf stems are armed with long spines. The fruit is orangish brown.

Care: This slow-growing palm does well in either alkaline or acidic soils high in organic matter. It appreciates regular water and develops no nutrient deficiencies if fed regularly. The plant tolerates brief dry spells and has fair salt tolerance. It is mildly susceptible to lethal yellowing. Insect pests are rarely a problem.

Recommended uses: Senegal date palm makes an exquisite focal point. It can stand on its own, but it also looks natural in a planting bed with lots of other foliage plants. Try trimming away the young suckers, leaving 6 to 15 stems that arch away from each other.

Phoenix roebelenii
FEE-nix ro-beh-LEEN-ee-eye
Pygmy date palm

- **Size: 12–15'H×6–8'W**
- **Light: Light shade to full sun**
- **Water: Drought tolerant to low**
- **Minimum temperature: 30°F**
- **Features: Single-trunk feather-leaf palm with spines**

Pygmy date palm

Pygmy date palm grows along rivers and streams in Laos, Vietnam, and southern China. The 3- to 5-inch-thick trunk is covered in old leaf bases and fibers except in its oldest part, which displays knobby leaf scars. The 3- to 5-foot-long shiny dark green leaves are made up of leaflets borne along stems armed with long spines. The fruit is jet black. **Care:** This palm does best in acidic to neutral soil but tolerates somewhat alkaline soil containing a moderate amount of organic matter. It needs regular water and fertilizer. Plants grown in highly alkaline soil sometimes develop a manganese deficiency, and those not fed regularly may have a potassium deficiency. Pygmy date palm has no major disease or pest problems. It is not very salt-tolerant. Indoors the plant needs bright light. **Recommended uses:** The plant's compact size makes it versatile. Use it as a small focal point either on its own or surrounded by other foliage plants. It makes a delightful container plant outdoors or indoors.

Phoenix sylvestris
FEE-nix sil-VES-tris
Silver date palm

- **Size: 45–55'H×20–25'W**
- **Light: Full sun**
- **Water: Drought tolerant to low**
- **Minimum temperature: 25°F**
- **Features: Single-trunk feather-leaf palm with bluish leaves**

This palm is native to India and Pakistan. The 18-inch-diameter trunk is covered in old leaf bases that form a beautiful crisscross pattern when they are trimmed. The 8- to 10-foot-long leaves are silver blue to bluish green, and long spines line the leaf stems. The fruit is purplish black. **Care:** Silver date palm grows well in acidic to somewhat alkaline soil that drains well. The plant appreciates regular water and fertilizer. It withstands brief dry periods, and its salt tolerance is fair. Lethal yellowing and fusarium wilt can be a concern. Insect pests are seldom a problem. **Recommended uses:** Use silver date palm in much the same way as date palm and Canary Island date palm except at a slightly smaller scale. It will not overwhelm a small landscape. Because it comes from a wetter native habitat than its two larger cousins, it is better suited to high-rainfall regions such as the Gulf Coast—and in those areas it maintains a fuller crown than either of its cousins.

Silver date palm

Phytelephas macrocarpa
feye-TEL-eh-fas mak-ro-KARP-uh
Vegetable ivory palm

- **Size: 12–15'H×8–12'W**
- **Light: Moderate shade**
- **Water: Moderate to wet**
- **Minimum temperature: 32°F**
- **Features: Single-trunk feather-leaf palm with subterranean trunk**

Vegetable ivory palm

Native to the wet rain forests of Peru, Brazil, and Bolivia, this palm has an underground trunk—all you see is the crown of 10- to 15-foot-long medium to dark green leaves on brownish leaf stems. The brown fruit, each containing one to four seeds, is borne on clublike stems. The extremely hard ivorylike seeds, used as a substitute for elephant ivory, are carved into buttons, figurines, and other art objects. Only a female plant produces seed, and a male plant must be nearby to pollinate it. **Care:** This palm prefers moist acidic to neutral soil. It is not drought tolerant; its roots require a plentiful water supply. The plant likes regular feeding and has no major nutrient, disease, or insect pest problems. It does not tolerate salt in the soil or air. **Recommended uses:** Vegetable ivory palm is a graceful addition to a wet, shady, rain forest-type garden. Remember, if you want to grow this plant for its seeds you'll have to plant both a female and a male plant.

Pigafetta elata
pig-uh-FET-uh ee-LAHT-uh

Wanga palm

- **Size:** 50–70'H×15–20'W
- **Light:** Full sun
- **Water:** Moderate to wet
- **Minimum temperature:** 35°F
- **Features:** Single-trunk feather-leaf palm covered in sharp spines

Wanga palm

Wanga palm can reach a height of more than 100 feet but generally is smaller in cultivation. This native of Indonesia develops a 12- to 18-inch-thick trunk that is dull green in its newer part. The deep olive green leaves arch beautifully and all parts of the leaf are covered in black spines. The small scaly fruit is brownish orange when ripe.

Care: This is one of the fastest-growing palms. It needs soil with some organic matter mixed in and lots of water. It will not tolerate dry or salty conditions. Regular fertilizer will help maintain robust growth. The plant has no major disease problems. Spider mites are an occasional problem when wanga palm is small.

Recommended uses: Once it becomes tall enough this extremely regal palm creates a wonderful silhouette against the sky. Plant several in a group to achieve the desired effect. Because wanga palm grows so tall and so fast, locate it where you can view it from a distance.

Pinanga caesia
pih-NAN-guh see-zee-uh

Pinanga caesia

- **Size:** 12–15'H×6–8'W
- **Light:** Moderate to light shade
- **Water:** Moderate
- **Minimum temperature:** 35°F
- **Features:** Single-trunk feather-leaf palm with orangish crownshaft

An understory rain forest palm from Sulawesi, an Indonesian island, this species has a trunk that grows to 3 inches thick and is topped with a brownish orange crownshaft. In young plants the leaves can be mottled and the newly emerging growth reddish, but the foliage usually turns deep green with a slightly bluish tint as the palm matures. The arching leaves reach 5 to 6 feet long. The ripe fruit is deep red.

Care: This moderate grower prefers humusy, well-drained acidic soil. The plant needs regular water; it will not tolerate dry soil conditions. Avoid nutrient deficiencies by fertilizing regularly. It does not appreciate full sun or salt. Pests and diseases pose no major problems.

Recommended uses: Locate this palm where you can enjoy it at close range. For the best effect put it under a high canopy with other understory plants.

Pinanga caesia

Pinanga coronata
pih-NAN-guh kor-o-NAHT-uh

Ivory cane palm

- **Size:** 15–20'H×12–15'W
- **Light:** Heavy to moderate shade
- **Water:** Moderate
- **Minimum temperature:** 32°F
- **Features:** Multitrunk feather-leaf palm with ivory crownshaft

Ivory cane palm

This native of Indonesia is often listed as *P. kuhlii*. The green trunks are about 2 inches thick. The light yellowish or ivory crownshaft contrasts beautifully with the medium to dark green leaves; the newly emerging growth is light pink. Each leaf has irregularly spaced leaflets of variable width. The fruit is black.

Care: Ivory cane palm prefers well-drained acidic soil but tolerates alkaline soil. The plant needs regular water; it does not tolerate dry conditions well. It has no salt tolerance. The palm grows at a moderate rate and has no major pest or disease problems.

Recommended uses: Plant ivory cane palm where you can view its contrasting crownshaft color and pink new growth. It grows best under the shade of larger trees and works well in a planting area combined with other foliage plants. The dense foliage can be used as a screen. Also consider it for use in a large container in a covered outdoor area.

Pinanga dicksonii
pih-NAN-guh dik-SO-nee-eye
Ivory crownshaft palm

- **Size: 15–20'H×12–15'W**
- **Light: Heavy to light shade**
- **Water: Moderate**
- **Minimum temperature: 32°F**
- **Features: Multitrunk feather-leaf palm with ivory crownshaft**

Ivory crownshaft palm

A densely clumping palm from India, ivory crownshaft palm has 2-inch-thick trunks that are deep green except in their oldest parts, which have prominent leaf scar rings. The golden ivory crownshaft is topped by 3- to 4-foot-long leaves of medium to dark green. The fruit is deep red.
Care: This palm, which grows at a moderate pace, succeeds in acidic or alkaline soil containing some organic matter. The plant needs regular water; it does not tolerate drought or salt. Occasional extra nitrogen or regular feeding with a high-nitrogen fertilizer will keep it at its greenest. This palm has slightly more sun tolerance than other palms in the genus.
Recommended uses: A beautiful palm like this—its contrasting crownshaft color gives it added appeal—deserves a spot where it can be appreciated up close. But it needs some space around it to show off best. It also makes a gorgeous screening plant, either alone or in a grouping.

Pinanga maculata
pih-NAN-guh mak-yoo-LAHT-uh
Tiger palm

- **Size: 10–15'H×5–7'W**
- **Light: Heavy to moderate shade**
- **Water: Moderate**
- **Minimum temperature: 35°F**
- **Features: Single-trunk feather-leaf palm with purplish crownshaft**

Tiger palm is a delicate-looking native of the Philippines. The trunk grows no larger than 2 inches thick and is topped by a brownish purple crownshaft. The 4-foot-long leaves are deep green on top and light silver underneath; young plants may develop mottled leaves. The leaves are divided into wide leaflets that are deeply divided on the ends.
Care: This is a true rain forest palm that appreciates lots of shade and does not tolerate drought. The plant prefers humusy acidic to neutral soil that drains well. It does not like salt-laden winds. Moderately fast-growing tiger palm needs only regular fertilizer. It has no major disease or insect pest problems.
Recommended uses: Locate this gorgeous palm where you can view it up close—for example, as an intimate specimen under a high canopy with other lush foliage around it.

Tiger palm crownshaft

Pritchardia hillebrandii
pritch-ARD-ee-uh hil-eh-BRAND-ee-eye
Dwarf pritchardia

- **Size: 15–20'H×8–10'W**
- **Light: Full sun**
- **Water: Moderate**
- **Minimum temperature: 30°F**
- **Features: Single-trunk fan-leaf palm with stiff green or bluish leaves**

Dwarf pritchardia

Native to Hawaii dwarf pritchardia comes in green and silvery blue forms. The hemispherical leaves, to 4 feet across, range from grassy green to silvery blue on top but always have some silver on the underside. The gray trunk is 8 to 10 inches in diameter. The spherical marble-size fruit is black when mature.
Care: A slow to moderate grower, dwarf pritchardia does well in either acidic or alkaline soil that drains well. It prefers regular water and without regular fertilizer it may develop a potassium deficiency. Insect pests are not normally a problem, but the plant is highly susceptible to lethal yellowing. It tolerates salt well.
Recommended uses: Use this picturesque palm on its own as a focal point. A grouping of several dwarf pritchardias of varying heights is also superb. A low dark green groundcover at the base of the plant creates a wonderful contrast with the silvery foliage.

Pritchardia pacifica
pritch-ARD-ee-uh puh-SIF-ih-kuh
Fiji fan palm

- **Size: 30–35'H×10–12'W**
- **Light: Full sun**
- **Water: Moderate**
- **Minimum temperature: 32°F**
- **Features: Single-trunk fan-leaf palm with bright green flat leaves**

Fiji fan palm

This Tonga native has a foot-thick gray trunk that is usually bulbous at the base. The 4- to 6-foot-wide semicircular leaves are grassy green, and the leaf stems are covered with a white waxy coating. The fruit is shiny black. **Care:** Fiji fan palm, which grows at a moderate rate, is equally at home in well-drained acidic or alkaline soil. It likes regular water and fertilizer. An occasional potassium deficiency is easy to correct with supplemental potassium fertilizer. This plant's salt tolerance is good. Insect pests are not usually a problem, but this palm is highly susceptible to lethal yellowing. **Recommended uses:** Although Fiji fan palm makes a fine specimen, it is best used in a large grouping at staggered heights. Mulch the area under and around a grove or plant a low contrasting groundcover to accent the palm's beauty. This palm is a perfect companion for Thurston palm.

Pritchardia thurstonii
pritch-ARD-ee-uh thur-STOHN-ee-eye
Thurston palm

- **Size: 30–35'H×10–12'W**
- **Light: Full sun**
- **Water: Moderate**
- **Minimum temperature: 30°F**
- **Features: Single-trunk fan-leaf palm with long fruit cluster**

This palm comes from Fiji, where it can grow to 50 feet or more. The 8-inch-diameter trunk is gray. The 4- to 6-foot-wide leaves are medium to dark green, and the leaf stems have a white waxy coating. The yellow flower clusters extend well beyond the leaves and arch down. The small round fruit is black when mature. **Care:** Moderately fast-growing Thurston palm does well in either well-drained acidic or alkaline soil. The plant prefers regular water but tolerates short periods of drought. A potassium deficiency may develop if the plant is not fertilized regularly. This palm is highly susceptible to lethal yellowing. Insect pests are rarely a problem, and the plant's salt tolerance is good. **Recommended uses:** Use Thurston palm in the same ways as Fiji fan palm. Consider planting the two species together.

Thurston palm

Pseudophoenix sargentii
soo-doh-FEE-nix sar-JEN-tee-eye
Buccaneer palm, Cherry palm

- **Size: 10–15'H×7–9'W**
- **Light: Full sun**
- **Water: Drought tolerant**
- **Minimum temperature: 28°F**
- **Features: Single-trunk feather-leaf palm with short crownshaft**

Buccaneer palm

Buccaneer palm comes from the Caribbean. The lower part of the trunk can be 12 inches thick but shrinks to 6 inches or less at eye level. It is light gray in the older section to waxy gray green in the newer part. The crownshaft is waxy bluish green, and the 6- to 8-foot-long leaves are also bluish green. The ripe, cherry red fruit is the source of the plant's other common name. **Care:** This very slow-growing palm thrives in fast-draining rocky or sandy soil that is alkaline. It prefers light watering and tolerates drought well. Its salt tolerance is excellent. The plant has no major disease or pest problems. **Recommended uses:** Buccaneer palm resembles a small royal palm and is ideal in a small landscape where a massive royal palm would be out of place. The plant is especially striking planted in groups. There is no need to add other foliage plants around it, although it combines well with succulent plants such as agaves and cacti.

Pseudophoenix vinifera
soo-doh-FEE-nix vin-IF-er-uh

Cherry palm, Wine palm

- **Size:** 35–40'H×12–15'W
- **Light:** Full sun
- **Water:** Drought tolerant to low
- **Minimum temperature:** 30°F
- **Features:** Single-trunk feather-leaf palm with short crownshaft

Cherry palm

Cherry palm is native to Hispaniola, where it grows to 70 feet or more. The smooth whitish trunk has an elongated bottle shape that narrows in older specimens. At its widest the trunk can be 18 inches thick. The crownshaft and lower leaf stems are covered in white wax. The deep green leaves, which grow 10 to 12 feet long, arch gracefully. The fruit is brilliant red.

Care: This slow-growing palm prefers alkaline to neutral soil that drains freely. Regular light watering and regular feeding will keep the plant growing robustly. It has no major disease or pest problems, and it tolerates short dry periods well. Its salt tolerance is good.

Recommended uses: Cherry palm makes an excellent specimen or group planting. Keep it clear of any tall plants that may obscure its showy trunk. Instead surround it with a groundcover or low-growing shrubs.

Ptychosperma elegans
teye-ko-SPURM-uh EL-eh-gunz

Solitaire palm

- **Size:** 25–30'H×8–10'W
- **Light:** Full sun
- **Water:** Drought tolerant to low
- **Minimum temperature:** 30°F
- **Features:** Single-trunk feather-leaf palm with crownshaft

A widely cultivated species from Australia, solitaire palm has a 4-inch-thick smooth gray trunk topped by a grayish green crownshaft. The arched leaves are deep emerald green on top and slightly lighter green underneath. Each V-shape leaf is 4 to 6 feet long. The small fruit is crimson.

Care: This palm does well in acidic or alkaline soil that drains well. It prefers regular water and fertilizer. The plant has some salt tolerance. Mealybugs occasionally infest the bud, leading to the development of sooty mold on the leaves. Nutrient and disease problems are rare.

Recommended uses: Solitaire palm looks best in multiples. You can even plant several to form a single clump; the individual palms will arch gracefully away from each other, creating a beautiful effect. The plant is also excellent as a background palm or for visually softening the corners of a home. It adds a graceful tropical feel around the pool and patio.

Solitaire palm

Ptychosperma macarthurii
teye-ko-SPURM-uh mak-ar-THUR-ee-eye

Macarthur palm

- **Size:** 30–35'H×15–20'W
- **Light:** Light shade to full sun
- **Water:** Drought tolerant to low
- **Minimum temperature:** 30°F
- **Features:** Multitrunk feather-leaf palm with crownshaft

Macarthur palm

This rain forest native of New Guinea and Australia creates a large clump when conditions suit it. The 2-inch-wide trunks are smooth and gray. The crownshaft is lighter green than the slightly arched leaves, which are medium to deep green. Each leaf grows 3 to 6 feet long. The tree nearly always bears fruit, which ripens to scarlet and contributes color year-round.

Care: Macarthur palm grows well in acidic or alkaline soil containing some organic matter. Its growth rate is moderate when it is fertilized and watered regularly. It has only a slight salt tolerance. Mealybugs occasionally infest the crown, which leads to the development of sooty mold on the leaves. The plant has no major disease or nutrient problems.

Recommended uses: Use this palm as a specimen to show off its clusters of red fruit. It also makes an excellent screening plant or a background for other palms or foliage plants.

Ptychosperma waitianum
teye-ko-SPURM-uh way-tee-AHN-um
Red leaf palm

- **Size:** 10–12'H×5–7'W
- **Light:** Moderate to light shade
- **Water:** Moderate
- **Minimum temperature:** 32°F
- **Features:** Multitrunk feather-leaf palm with crownshaft

Red leaf palm

This rain forest native of New Guinea has trunks no more than an inch in diameter. They are green but change to brown in the older parts. The 2- to 3-foot-long leaves have triangular leaflets. Newly emerging leaves are salmon red turning glossy medium to dark green. The crownshaft is lighter green with a sprinkling of white waxy fuzz. The ripe fruit is black.

Care: This palm grows well in moist acidic to neutral soil that drains well. Its growth rate is slow to moderate, and it responds well to regular water and fertilizer. The plant does not tolerate drought or salt. Insect pests and diseases are infrequent.

Recommended uses: Give this dainty-looking palm a spot where you can appreciate it at close range—it really stands out when its colorful new leaves unfurl. It's most effective planted with other contrasting foliage plants under a high canopy.

Raphia farinifera
RAF-ee-uh far-ih-NIF-er-uh
Raffia palm

- **Size:** 60–80'H×25–30'W
- **Light:** Full sun
- **Water:** Wet to aquatic
- **Minimum temperature:** 32°F
- **Features:** Single- or multitrunk feather-leaf palm

Native to Uganda, Kenya, and Tanzania, this large palm generally has one to three trunks—each can be as much as 2 feet thick—that are covered in old leaf bases. The immense leaves can reach 80 feet long but usually are shorter. Both the leaf bases and leaf stems are orange. The long leaflets are dark green on top and bluish green underneath. The scaly fruit is brown.

Care: Moderately fast-growing raffia palm prefers acidic or alkaline soil containing some organic matter. The plant needs wet conditions and does not tolerate drought. It demonstrates its dislike for drier situations by developing brown leaf tips and short leaves. It has no nutrient problems as long as it receives regular fertilizer. Palm aphids and the resulting sooty mold occasionally become a problem. The plant has no major disease problems and is not salt-tolerant.

Recommended uses: This impressive palm is best used as a specimen in a wet area or on the bank of a water feature.

Raffia palm

Ravenea hildebrandtii
ruh-VEN-ee-uh hil-deh-BRANT-ee-eye
Dwarf majesty palm

- **Size:** 8–10'H×5–7'W
- **Light:** Moderate shade
- **Water:** Moderate
- **Minimum temperature:** 30°F
- **Features:** Single-trunk feather-leaf palm with medium green leaves

Dwarf majesty palm

Dwarf majesty palm is native to the Comoros, a group of islands off the coast of Africa near Madagascar. It is an understory rain forest palm with a 2-inch-thick trunk that is tan to brown. The 2- to 3-foot-long leaves are medium grassy green. The tiny fruit is bright orange at maturity.

Care: This small palm, which grows at a moderate rate, does well in humusy acidic or alkaline soil that drains well. It prefers regular water and is not drought-resistant. Nutrient deficiencies are rare with regular feeding. The plant is slightly susceptible to lethal yellowing, but insect pests rarely bother it. Its salt tolerance is low.

Recommended uses: A single dwarf majesty palm under a high canopy with other contrasting foliage plants will become a focal point in the garden. This palm is also a perfect candidate for containers on a patio or porch.

Ravenea rivularis
ruh-VEN-ee-uh riv-yoo-LAR-is

Majesty palm, Majestic palm

- **Size: 40–50'H×10–12'W**
- **Light: Full sun**
- **Water: Moderate to wet**
- **Minimum temperature: 30°F**
- **Features: Single-trunk feather-leaf palm with tan trunk**

Majesty palm

Majesty palm towers along rivers and streams in Madagascar, where it can grow to 80 feet tall. The tapering light tan to gray trunk can be 2 feet in diameter. The leaflets making up the 6- to 8-foot-long medium to dark green leaves are regularly spaced and held in a single plane. The tiny fruit is orangish red. **Care:** This palm grows equally well in acidic or alkaline soil but needs wet conditions. It hates any dry period. Give it plenty of water and fertilizer and majesty palm will reward you with fast growth. Diseases and insect pests are insignificant threats. The plant has no salt tolerance. **Recommended uses:** Majesty palm is ideal near water features. A grouping creates a magnificent backdrop along the bank of a pond. The plant's full spherical crown makes a wonderful silhouette against the sky, and it looks grand with other plants around its base. It is a popular container palm in the North, where it is treated like an annual.

Reinhardtia gracilis
ryne-HART-ee-uh gruh-SIL-is

Windowpane palm

- **Size: 5–7'H×3–4'W**
- **Light: Moderate shade**
- **Water: Moderate**
- **Minimum temperature: 32°F**
- **Features: Multitrunk feather-leaf palm with leaf windows**

This palm comes from Central America, where it grows as an understory rain forest plant. The knobby stems are about ½ inch thick and covered in old leaf bases in their newer sections. Each 6- to 12-inch-long bright green leaf is made up of four to eight leaflets with small openings or windows where they attach to the leaf stem. The fruit is shiny black when ripe. **Care:** Moderately fast-growing windowpane palm is rather particular about its growing conditions. The plant requires well-drained acidic soil containing some organic matter. It needs a constant supply of moisture and is partial to high humidity; it does not tolerate dryness. It likes regular fertilizer and is intolerant of salt. As long as its conditions are met, the plant has no pest, disease, or nutrient problems. **Recommended uses:** Windowpane palm needs an intimate garden spot where it can show off its beauty at close range. It stands out better when surrounded by other low-growing plants.

Windowpane palm

Rhapidophyllum hystrix
rap-id-o-FEYE-lum HISS-trix

Needle palm

- **Size: 8–12'H×5–7'W**
- **Light: Moderate to light shade**
- **Water: Moderate**
- **Minimum temperature: 20°F**
- **Features: Multitrunk fan-leaf palm with needlelike spines**

Needle palm

This swamp dweller from the southeastern United States is quite cold hardy. Its trunks are short and covered in fibers and old leaf bases. Emerging from the base of the leaf stems are spines 4 to 6 inches or longer. Leaves to 3 feet across are deep green on top with a silver cast underneath. The fruit is brownish. **Care:** Slow-growing needle palm flourishes in acidic or alkaline soil as long as it contains some organic matter. It does not tolerate drought and has only slight salt tolerance. The plant needs regular water and fertilizer. Although this palm tolerates full sun, it looks best in moderate shade. Insect pests and disease problems are infrequent. **Recommended uses:** This palm looks best in the company of other plants. Under a high canopy its dark green leaves contrast beautifully with other shade-tolerant foliage plants. Place it out of pedestrian traffic flow.

Rhapis excelsa
RAP-is ek-SEL-suh

Lady palm

- **Size:** 8–10'H×8–10'W
- **Light:** Heavy to light shade
- **Water:** Moderate
- **Minimum temperature:** 25°F
- **Features:** Multitrunk fan-leaf palm with bright green leaves

Lady palm

Never found in the wild, lady palm may have originated in southern China. Many cultivars, including unusual variegated versions developed in Japan, are available. They vary in size and leaf shape, but all form dense clumps. The trunks are no more than an inch thick and are covered in black fibers. The leaves, about a foot wide, are glossy dark green. The clump width is virtually unlimited because the plant spreads by rhizomes (horizontally creeping underground stems). The mature fruit is white.

Care: Slow-growing lady palm thrives in acidic to somewhat alkaline soil containing some organic matter. It prefers regular water and fertilizer. Its drought and salt tolerances are low. The plant tolerates some sun but maintains better color in shade. Nutrient problems, diseases, and insect pests are seldom a concern.

Recommended uses: Lady palm makes an excellent privacy screen and excels in planters. As a container palm for patio or indoors it has no equal.

Rhapis humilis
RAP-is HYOO-mih-lis

Slender lady palm

- **Size:** 12–15'H×12–15'W
- **Light:** Heavy to light shade
- **Water:** Moderate
- **Minimum temperature:** 22°F
- **Features:** Multitrunk fan-leaf palm with deeply divided leaves

This palm's origin is unknown, though the nursery trade can trace its stock to plants originally cultivated in China. The trunks are an inch wide and covered in brownish black fibers. The leaves, measuring 18 inches across, are deep green. The leaf segments are thinner and longer than those of lady palm. There is no fruit because, despite the plant's common name, all plants sold are divisions from male plants.

Care: Slow-growing slender lady palm prefers acidic to neutral soil but tolerates alkaline soil if some organic matter has been incorporated. The plant performs best with regular water and fertilizer. It tolerates brief drought periods but has little salt tolerance. This palm has no major nutrient, disease, or pest problems.

Recommended uses: Slender lady palm is an excellent screening plant to hide an unsightly view or break up a blank space. Plant it in front of a light-colored wall to show off its graceful form. This palm is also a superb container plant for indoor or outdoor use; as the clump enlarges it will fill the pot beautifully.

Slender lady palm

Rhapis subtilis
RAP-is SUB-tih-lis

Dwarf lady palm

- **Size:** 2–7'H×2–7'W
- **Light:** Heavy to moderate shade
- **Water:** Moderate
- **Minimum temperature:** 30°F
- **Features:** Multitrunk fan-leaf palm with variable leaf shape

Dwarf lady palm

Dwarf lady palm is a highly variable species native to Cambodia, Laos, and Thailand. The trunks are generally ½ inch thick and covered in brown to black fibers. The height and width range from 2 to 7 feet. The 6- to 10-inch-wide leaves are divided into segments that vary in number, from 3 to 12, as well as width. The white fruit is one of the few consistent features of this palm.

Care: Slow-growing dwarf lady palm does best in humusy acidic to slightly alkaline soil. The plant likes regular watering and feeding. It cannot tolerate drought or salt. Nutrient deficiencies are rare, as are pest and disease problems.

Recommended uses: It seems that no two plants of this species are exactly alike, which makes each one a unique treasure. Some make lovely intimate specimens for close viewing, and others are best used against a blank backdrop to show off the silhouette of the variable leaves.

Rhopalostylis baueri
ro-pal-o-STY-lis BAU-er-eye
Norfolk Island palm

- **Size:** 30–35'H×8–10'W
- **Light:** Moderate to light shade
- **Water:** Moderate
- **Minimum temperature:** 28°F
- **Features:** Single-trunk feather-leaf palm with crownshaft

Norfolk Island palm

This palm is native to Norfolk and Raoul islands in the South Pacific, where it can grow to 50 feet or higher. The 8-inch-thick trunk is green in its younger portion changing to gray in its older part. It has a noticeably swollen crownshaft that is light green to yellowish green. The 10- to 12-foot-long ascending leaves are medium to dark green. The fruit is reddish brown.
Care: Norfolk Island palm can succeed in either acidic to slightly alkaline soil as long as it drains well. With regular water and fertilizer it grows at a moderate rate. It tolerates brief dry periods and is slightly salt-tolerant. The plant prefers cool nights. Nutrient problems seldom develop, and disease and pest problems are rare.
Recommended uses: This palm looks best when several are planted in a group, with or without other plants surrounding it. Make certain that any companion plants are short enough so they don't detract from the striking silhouette of the palm's crown.

Rhopalostylis sapida
ro-pal-o-STY-lis SAP-ih-duh
Nikau palm

- **Size:** 25–30'H×10–12'W
- **Light:** Moderate to light shade
- **Water:** Moderate
- **Minimum temperature:** 28°F
- **Features:** Single-trunk feather-leaf palm with crownshaft

Native to New Zealand and the nearby Chatham Islands, nikau palm has an 8-inch-diameter trunk that is green in its newer part to gray in its older section. The crownshaft is light lime green and much more bulbous than the closely related Norfolk Island palm. The 12- to 16-foot-long deep green leaves stiffly ascend, giving the appearance of a large feather duster. The fruit is red.
Care: This moderately slow-growing palm prefers well-drained acidic soil but tolerates slightly alkaline conditions. It shows no nutrient deficiencies as long as it gets regular fertilizer. The plant likes regular water but can handle short dry periods. It has some salt tolerance. This palm prefers cool nights. Insect pests and diseases are of no major concern.
Recommended uses: This tropical-looking palm is at home in a setting incorporating other lush foliage plants. It is handsome as a specimen and equally picturesque in groupings.

Nikau palm

Roystonea regia
roy-STOHN-ee-uh REE-jee-uh
Royal palm

- **Size:** 60–90'H×15–20'W
- **Light:** Full sun
- **Water:** Moderate
- **Minimum temperature:** 30°F
- **Features:** Single-trunk feather-leaf palm with crownshaft

Royal palm

From Florida and the Caribbean, royal palm has a smooth grayish white trunk that reaches 2 feet in diameter. It is generally columnar, although sometimes it develops a distinct bulge midway up the trunk. The deep green crownshaft can be 6 feet long. The 12-foot-long feathery leaves are bright green. The fruit is purplish black when ripe.
Care: Royal palm does well in soil that is acidic or alkaline and contains some organic matter. It thrives on regular water and fertilizer. Diseases are rare, but potassium deficiency is a sometimes fatal problem when royal palm grows in sandy soils. The royal palm bug, a sucking insect, can cause leaves to brown in winter and spring. The plant is not tolerant of drought or salt.
Recommended uses: Overpowering in a small landscape but magnificent in a large garden, royal palm is equally adapted to formal or casual tropical landscapes. It excels as a street tree or in a grouping of varied heights.

Sabal causiarum
SAY-bahl kau-see-AHR-um
Puerto Rican hat palm

- **Size: 45–60'H×15–18'W**
- **Light: Full sun**
- **Water: Drought tolerant to low**
- **Minimum temperature: 25°F**
- **Features: Single-trunk fan-leaf palm with massive columnar trunk**

Puerto Rican hat palm

When fully grown, this palm native to Puerto Rico and Hispaniola is one of the most majestic of all palms. Its smooth columnar trunk is nearly white and can reach 3 feet thick. The 5- to 6-foot-wide bluish green or deep green leaves are costapalmate, meaning they're shaped like the palm of a hand but with a leaf midrib in the center. The small fruit is jet black. This palm derives its common name from the fine-quality hats made from the leaves.

Care: Slow-growing Puerto Rican hat palm can succeed in either acidic or alkaline soil that drains well. It prefers regular water and fertilizer. The plant has fair salt tolerance and can handle short periods of drought. Diseases, insects, and nutrient deficiencies are not a problem for this palm.

Recommended uses: A mature Puerto Rican hat palm is impressive in a formal garden. It also makes an excellent street tree. Although this palm can overwhelm a small landscape, in the right setting a grouping is magnificent. It looks best where it won't dwarf other plants in the landscape.

Sabal mauritiiformis
SAY-bahl mau-rit-tee-eye-FOR-mis
Belize thatch palm

- **Size: 45–50'H×8–10'W**
- **Light: Full sun**
- **Water: Drought tolerant to low**
- **Minimum temperature: 30°F**
- **Features: Single-trunk fan-leaf palm with deeply divided leaves**

The leaves of this palm are commonly used as roofing thatch in its native habitat of Belize, Mexico, and Guatemala. The 8- to 10-inch-diameter trunk holds onto the old leaf bases until the palm is quite mature. These leaf bases remain green for several years. The leaves are circular with deeply divided segments, though on young plants the divisions aren't as deep. The foliage is deep green on top and silvery green underneath. The small fruit is shiny black at maturity.

Care: Belize thatch palm is equally at home in acidic or alkaline soil containing some organic matter. It grows at a moderate pace and does best with regular water and fertilizer. Its tolerance for salt is poor. Nutrient deficiencies are not a major problem, and few diseases or pests affect the plant.

Recommended uses: Even as a young plant Belize thatch palm is a beautiful addition to the landscape. It excels as a single plant but prefers the company of other palms, shrubs, and foliage plants in a rain forest-style garden.

Belize thatch palm

Sabal minor
SAY-bahl MY-nor
Dwarf palmetto palm

- **Size: 6–10'H×6–8'W**
- **Light: Full sun**
- **Water: Drought tolerant**
- **Minimum temperature: 20°F**
- **Features: Single-trunk fan-leaf palm with no upright trunk**

Dwarf palmetto palm

Native to Florida, Georgia, and west to Texas and Northeast Mexico, dwarf palmetto palm generally has an underground trunk, although it can develop an aboveground trunk to 10 feet tall. The leaves, measuring 3 to 4 feet across, are deep green to slightly bluish green. The small shiny black fruit grows in a stiffly erect cluster.

Care: This slow-growing palm flourishes in acidic or alkaline soil that drains well. It is drought-tolerant, but prefers light watering and regular feeding. The plant has good salt tolerance. It prefers full sun but can grow in light shade. No diseases or pests bother it, and nutrient deficiencies are rare.

Recommended uses: Dwarf palmetto palm looks awkward and out of place on its own; plant several of them together. It is striking when treated as a shrub in a planting bed with other foliage plants.

Sabal palmetto
SAY-bahl palm-ET-o

Cabbage palm, Palmetto

- **Size: 50–70'H×10–12'W**
- **Light: Full sun**
- **Water: Drought tolerant**
- **Minimum temperature: 22°F**
- **Features: Single-trunk fan-leaf palm with deep khaki green leaves**

Cabbage palm

Cabbage palm originates in the southeastern United States, the Bahamas, and Cuba. Its trunk is 12 to 16 inches thick and covered with old leaf bases that persist until the palm gets rather old. The leaf bases make nice points of attachment for orchids and bromeliads. The deep olive green leaves are 3 to 4 feet wide and deeply costapalmate (shaped like the palm of a hand but with a leaf midrib in the center). The small fruit is black. The heart is sometimes called swamp cabbage.

Care: This slow grower does well in either acidic or alkaline soil that drains well. Although the plant is drought-tolerant, it thrives on regular light watering and regular feeding. It is highly tolerant of salt winds, but not saltwater flooding. Nutrient, disease, and pest problems are rare.

Recommended uses: Cabbage palm displays a handsome form as a specimen, but it also looks good in a grouping. It can stand on its own or serve as a canopy for lower-growing plants.

Salacca zalacca
suh-LAK-uh zuh-LAK-uh

Salak palm

- **Size: 10–15'H×15–20'W**
- **Light: Moderate to light shade**
- **Water: Wet**
- **Minimum temperature: 35°F**
- **Features: Multitrunk feather-leaf palm with spiny leaf stems**

Native to Sumatra and Java, this trunkless palm forms a dense clump of upright leaves with spiny leaf stems. The leaflets—glossy green on top and silvery underneath—are arranged in groups along the stem and radiate out in all directions, giving the leaf a feathery appearance. The scaly fruit is reddish brown. Several cultivars are commercially produced for the savory fruit, which is sold in Asian markets.

Care: Salak palm prefers acidic to neutral soil with some organic matter mixed in. It requires constant moisture to thrive. With regular fertilizer the plant grows quite fast. It does not tolerate salt. The plant seldom suffers nutrient deficiencies, and any disease and insect pest problems are usually insignificant.

Recommended uses: This palm is quite ornamental when used with contrasting plants that show off its striking foliage. Locate the plant where you can appreciate the foliage up close and watch the shiny green top and silvery undersides dancing in the breeze.

Salak palm ripe fruits

Satakentia liukiuensis
sat-uh-KENT-ee-uh lee-oo-kee-oo-EN-sis

Satake palm

- **Size: 45–50'H×12–15'W**
- **Light: Full sun**
- **Water: Moderate**
- **Minimum temperature: 30°F**
- **Features: Single-trunk feather-leaf palm with purplish crownshaft**

Satake palm crownshaft

Satake palm comes from the Ryukyu Islands of Japan. Its light brownish trunk is 10 to 12 inches in diameter and is topped with a crownshaft of shiny deep purple. The crownshaft is especially evident when the oldest leaf has just peeled away. The 8- to 10-foot-long arched leaves are made up of glossy deep green leaflets held in a single plane. The tiny fruit is reddish black.

Care: This palm does well in either acidic or alkaline soil that drains well. It needs regular water and fertilizer for strong growth. An established plant withstands short periods of drought. Satake palm's salt tolerance is fair. Nutrient deficiencies, insect pests, and diseases are not a problem.

Recommended uses: Satake palm excels as a specimen in an open space, where its gracefulness will make it a focal point. A small grouping is equally attractive. A low groundcover at the palm's base will be effective.

Serenoa repens
ser-eh-NO-uh REP-enz
Saw palmetto

- **Size: 8–15'H×8–20'W**
- **Light: Light shade to full sun**
- **Water: Drought tolerant**
- **Minimum temperature: 22°F**
- **Features: Multitrunk fan-leaf palm with branching trunks**

Saw palmetto

This native of the southeastern United States is variable. Its branching trunks generally grow underground or recline on the ground, but they can be upright. They are covered in old leaf bases and have a diameter of 6 to 8 inches. The 2- to 3-foot-wide leaves are olive to bluish green, except for a unique form from the eastern coast of Florida that is whitish silver. The leaf stems are armed with tiny teeth on both sides. The yellowish black fruit is reportedly helpful in treating prostate problems.

Care: Slow-growing saw palmetto takes either acidic or alkaline soil that drains well. It is drought tolerant but likes regular light watering. The plant is salt tolerant. It has few nutrient problems and disease and pest problems are rare.

Recommended uses: Saw palmetto can be used as a screening plant though it tends to sprawl. A large specimen makes a handsome focal point. You can also use this palm to completely fill a planting bed or as shrubs in light shade under tall trees.

Syagrus amara
sy-AG-rus uh-MAR-uh
Overtop palm

- **Size: 50–60'H×12–15'W**
- **Light: Full sun**
- **Water: Moderate**
- **Minimum temperature: 30°F**
- **Features: Single-trunk feather-leaf palm with dark green leaves**

This palm comes from the Lesser Antilles. The 10- to 12-inch-thick tan to light gray trunk is swollen at the base. The 10-foot-long leaves consist of deep green leaflets that tend to droop. The ripe fruit is orange.

Care: Moderately fast-growing overtop palm does best in acidic to somewhat alkaline soil; nutrient deficiencies sometimes occur when it is planted in highly alkaline soil. Regular water and fertilizer keeps the plant robust. Its drought tolerance is limited to short dry periods. This palm has some salt tolerance. It is not affected by any major disease or pest problems.

Recommended uses: The deep green foliage of overtop palm stands out in the landscape. This plant makes a great canopy palm when several are planted in a group. It looks natural in a rain forest setting with other palms and tropical foliage plants.

Overtop palm

Syagrus coronata
sy-AG-rus kor-o-NAHT-uh
Licury palm

- **Size: 25–35'H×12–15'W**
- **Light: Full sun**
- **Water: Drought tolerant**
- **Minimum temperature: 30°F**
- **Features: Single-trunk feather-leaf palm with spiraling trunk**

Licury palm

Licury palm is native to eastern Brazil, where its seeds are a primary food for the endangered hyacinth macaw. The trunk has a diameter of 8 to 10 inches and is covered with spirally arranged old leaf bases. The 10-foot-long feathery leaves are deep olive green on top and silvery green underneath. The fruit is orangish brown, and the edible seeds taste like coconut.

Care: This slow-grower likes well-drained soil but is not particular about whether it's acidic or alkaline. Although drought-tolerant the plant prefers regular light watering and regular feeding. It has fair salt tolerance. Nutrient deficiencies, diseases, and pest problems are rare.

Recommended uses: Licury palm looks good as a specimen or in a grouping of staggered heights. Position this palm where you'll have a good view of the attractive spiraling trunk. Avoid grouping plants around it but rather frame it from behind.

Syagrus romanzoffiana
sy-AG-rus ro-man-zof-ee-AHN-uh

Queen palm

- **Size: 50–60'H×15–18'W**
- **Light: Full sun**
- **Water: Drought tolerant to low**
- **Minimum temperature: 28°F**
- **Features: Single-trunk feather-leaf palm with smooth gray trunk**

Queen palm

This commonly cultivated palm is from southern Brazil, Paraguay, and Argentina. It is somewhat variable in size and leaf color. The gray trunk can grow anywhere from 10 to 20 inches thick. The 10- to 15-foot-long leaves are medium to dark green on top and lighter green to silvery green underneath. The fruit is bright orange; some types are sweet and delicious. Queen palm hybridizes easily with other species in its own genus as well as with species in the genus *Butia*.

Care: This palm, which grows at a moderate rate, prefers acidic to neutral soil that drains well. It suffers manganese deficiency in alkaline soils. The plant likes regular water and fertilizer. It has a slight tolerance for drought and salt. Diseases and pest problems are infrequent.

Recommended uses: The larger forms of queen palm are most impressive in the landscape. Use them alone or better yet in a grouping. They excel in planting beds with other foliage plants beneath them.

Syagrus schizophylla
sy-AG-rus skits-o-FEYE-luh

Arikury palm

- **Size: 10–12'H×5–7'W**
- **Light: Light shade to full sun**
- **Water: Drought tolerant**
- **Minimum temperature: 30°F**
- **Features: Single-trunk feather-leaf palm with deep green leaves**

This native of Brazil grows along the coast just inland from the ocean. The trunk is 4 to 6 inches wide and is covered in old leaf bases that are great places to attach epiphytic ferns, orchids, and bromeliads. The 5- to 6-foot-long leaves are divided into deep green leaflets arranged in a single plane. The leaf stems are armed with sharp teethlike projections. The fruit is bright orange.

Care: This palm prefers well-drained alkaline to slightly acidic soil. Regular light watering and regular feeding will usually keep it growing strongly, although it is quite susceptible to potassium deficiency. Excess water can cause bud rot to develop. The plant is also slightly susceptible to lethal yellowing. It has good drought and salt tolerance.

Recommended uses: Arikury palm makes an excellent container plant for the patio, and it can also be grown indoors. In the landscape it looks best combined with other foliage plants and positioned where it can be seen up close.

Arikury palm

Thrinax morrisii
THRY-nax mor-ISS-ee-eye

Key thatch palm

- **Size: 15–25'H×5–7'W**
- **Light: Full sun**
- **Water: Drought tolerant**
- **Minimum temperature: 28°F**
- **Features: Single-trunk fan-leaf palm with silvery leaf undersides**

Key thatch palm

Native to Florida and the Caribbean, this palm has a light gray trunk 6 to 8 inches thick. The 2- to 3-foot-wide leaves are yellowish green to medium green on top and bluish green to silver underneath. The leaf bases are split at the trunk, one characteristic that distinguishes it from *Coccothrinax*. The small fruit is white when it ripens.

Care: This very slow-growing palm prefers alkaline to slightly acidic soil that drains easily. The plant appreciates regular light watering and regular feeding. It has good drought and salt tolerance. Diseases and pests are not major problems. Nutrient deficiencies are rare on Key thatch palm.

Recommended uses: Key thatch palm looks attractive among other similar palms. A grouping of several at staggered heights is particularly pleasing. Plant low-growing ornamental grasses or flowering groundcovers underneath this palm to create a naturalistic combination.

Thrinax radiata
THRY-nax ray-dee-AHT-uh
Thatch palm

- **Size: 25–35'H×4–6'W**
- **Light: Full sun**
- **Water: Drought tolerant**
- **Minimum temperature: 30°F**
- **Features: Single-trunk fan-leaf palm with bright green leaves**

Thatch palm

As its name implies, thatch palm's foliage is used as roofing thatch. The plant is native to Florida and the Caribbean. The 4- to 5-inch-thick trunk is light gray, and the 3-foot-wide leaves are yellowish green to medium green. Small white fruit is borne in long clusters that extend beyond the leaves.

Care: Slow-growing thatch palm does well in alkaline to slightly acidic soil that drains well. It is drought-tolerant but prefers regular light watering and regular feeding. Nutritional deficiencies are rare with proper feeding. The plant has good salt tolerance and no major disease or pest problems.

Recommended uses: Plant multiples of thatch palms together; they'll arch away from one another in an attractive way. This palm also mixes well in a grouping of similar palms. It grows surprisingly well as an indoor plant when given adequate light.

Trachycarpus fortunei
tray-kee-KARP-us for-TOON-ee-eye
Windmill palm

- **Size: 30–35'H×5–7'W**
- **Light: Full sun**
- **Water: Drought tolerant to low**
- **Minimum temperature: 22°F**
- **Features: Single-trunk fan-leaf palm with brown trunk fibers**

Windmill palm is thought to be native to China, although its exact origin is unknown because of its long history of cultivation. The 8-inch-thick trunk is covered in brown fibers and old leaf bases except in its older section. The 3-foot-wide leaves are deep green. A yellow flower cluster on female plants eventually bears bluish black fruit.

Care: This moderately fast-growing palm succeeds in alkaline or acidic soil that drains well. Although it tolerates short dry periods, it does best when watered and fed regularly. The plant has fair salt tolerance. It rarely develops nutrient or pest problems. Windmill palm is mildly susceptible to lethal yellowing. It looks best when planted in an area protected from wind to prevent leaf tattering.

Recommended uses: A single specimen is an excellent focal point in a small landscape, but in a larger landscape several are better. Underplant this palm with other bold foliage plants to add a tropical feel to the garden.

Windmill palm

Trachycarpus wagnerianus
tray-kee-KARP-us wahg-ner-ee-AHN-us
Miniature Chusan palm

- **Size: 20–25'H×4–6'W**
- **Light: Full sun**
- **Water: Drought tolerant to low**
- **Minimum temperature: 22°F**
- **Features: Single-trunk fan-leaf palm with stiff leaves**

Miniature Chusan palm

Miniature Chusan palm was discovered in cultivation in Japan. It has never been found in the wild. The trunk is about 8 inches thick and is covered in a mat of brown fibers and old leaf bases. The fan-shape leaves are 18 to 24 inches wide and medium to dark green. The ripe fruit is bluish black.

Care: The soil can be acidic or alkaline as long as it drains well. Regular water and fertilizer will keep this slow to moderate grower thriving. The plant has moderate drought tolerance and slight salt tolerance. Nutrient problems are rare, and diseases and insect pests are not a threat. It grows best with cool night temperatures.

Recommended uses: When it's young this palm makes a picturesque accent in an intimate surrounding or an excellent container plant for the pool or patio. When it grows taller it develops a more compact crown and stiffer appearance; then it looks best planted in a grouping.

Trithrinax brasiliensis
try-THRY-nax bra-zil-ee-EN-sis
Spiny fiber palm

- **Size: 20–25'H×5–7'W**
- **Light: Light shade to full sun**
- **Water: Drought tolerant to low**
- **Minimum temperature: 28°F**
- **Features: Single-trunk fan-leaf palm with spiny fibers on trunk**

Spiny fiber palm; spiny trunk (inset)

Native to Brazil, this palm gets its common name from the brown fibers that cover the trunk and the rows of brown spines that arise from the old leaf bases. The trunk itself is seldom visible except in the oldest of plants. There it is about 6 inches in diameter. The 2- to 3-foot-wide leaves form a pleasing spiral pattern; they are deep green on top and silvery green underneath. The fruit is white.

Care: Spiny fiber palm grows well in well-drained acidic or alkaline soil. It tolerates dry periods but grows better when watered and fed regularly. Diseases, pests, and nutritional problems are insignificant. The plant is not salt-tolerant and does not grow well in the humid heat of South Florida; it prefers cool nights. In locations where it is adapted it is a moderately fast grower.

Recommended uses: This palm looks best combined with other foliage plants. However, choose a spot where you can view its unusual spiraling leaf pattern and interesting brown spiny fibers on the trunk.

Trithrinax campestris
try-THRY-nax kam-PES-tris
Blue needle palm

- **Size: 12–15'H×8–10'W**
- **Light: Full sun**
- **Water: Drought tolerant**
- **Minimum temperature: 13°F**
- **Features: Multitrunk fan-leaf palm with grayish green leaves**

A native of Argentina and Uruguay, blue needle palm has 4-inch-thick trunks covered in old leaf bases and spiny brown fibers. The 2-foot-wide leaves range from grayish green to silvery blue depending on the plant. The leaf segments are extremely rigid, and the leaf tips sharp enough to draw blood. The ripe fruit is white.

Care: This slow-growing palm wants well-drained soil that is either acidic or alkaline. It is somewhat drought-tolerant but likes regular light watering and regular feeding. Nutritional deficiencies are rare, and disease or insect pests seldom become a problem. This plant has some salt tolerance, and it prefers cool night temperatures.

Recommended uses: A clump of several blue needle palms is a striking focal point, but its sharp leaf tips make it dangerous to be around. Give the plant ample space and keep it away from walkways and heavily used areas. It looks handsome in a planting bed where the entire plant can be seen and admired.

Blue needle palm

Veitchia arecina
VEECH-ee-uh ar-eh-SEE-nuh
Sunshine palm

- **Size: 50–70'H×10–15'W**
- **Light: Full sun**
- **Water: Drought tolerant to low**
- **Minimum temperature: 29°F**
- **Features: Single-trunk feather-leaf palm with crownshaft**

Sunshine palm

This native of Vanuatu has a light grayish trunk that flares at the base but otherwise is 10 to 12 inches thick. The crownshaft is silvery green and more than 4 feet long. The 10- to 12-foot-long gently arching leaves bear slightly drooping deep emerald green leaflets. The crimson fruit is borne in large clusters.

Care: Fast-growing sunshine palm adapts to well-drained acidic or alkaline soil. It appreciates regular water, but an established plant can tolerate dry periods. Nutrient deficiencies are unusual. Lethal yellowing can be a problem, and mealybugs may occasionally infest the plant. The plant's salt tolerance is good.

Recommended uses: Sunshine palm is picturesque in groupings; a grove of the plants epitomizes the tropics. Although this palm doesn't need any companion plantings, it makes an attractive combination with other foliage plants under its canopy.

Verschaffeltia splendida
ver-shaf-ELT-ee-uh splen-DEED-uh
Stilt root palm

- **Size:** 20–25'H×8–10'W
- **Light:** Moderate to light shade
- **Water:** Moderate
- **Minimum temperature:** 32°F
- **Features:** Single-trunk feather-leaf palm with stilt roots

Stilt root palm; stilt roots (inset)

This rain forest palm is from the Seychelles, where it can reach 80 feet tall. It has unusual stilt roots (aboveground brace roots) that grow in a 3- to 4-foot-tall cone around the base of the gray trunk, which is 8 to 10 inches thick. The 6- to 8-foot-long leaves are generally undivided and resemble fish tails. Often the newly emerging growth is pinkish red before turning green. The leaf bases and leaf stems are covered in black spines. The fruit is brownish green.

Care: Stilt root palm prefers well-drained acidic to neutral soil containing some organic matter. It requires regular water and does not tolerate drought. Without regular fertilizer the plant may develop a potassium deficiency. It has no salt tolerance. Although it withstands full sun, it is usually placed in a protected area under a high canopy to prevent the wind from tattering the leaves. Disease and pest problems are rare.

Recommended uses: Wherever it is located stilt root palm becomes a focal point. Plant it where you can appreciate it at close range and from afar. Avoid obscuring the stilt roots with other foliage.

Wallichia disticha
wal-IK-ee-uh DIS-tik-uh
Traveler's palm

- **Size:** 25–30'H×10–12'W
- **Light:** Light shade to full sun
- **Water:** Moderate
- **Minimum temperature:** 28°F
- **Features:** Single-trunk feather-leaf palm with leaves in a single plane

Native to the Himalayan foothills, traveler's palm has an 8- to 10-inch-diameter trunk that, except in its oldest section, is covered with coarse brownish black fibers from old leaf bases. Its common name comes from the arrangement of leaves, which grow in a single plane, giving the palm a flattened appearance as though pointing in opposite compass directions. The 8- to 10-foot-long leaves are medium to dark green on top and silvery green underneath. The fruit contains a strong irritant; handle it with care.

Care: Traveler's palm prefers acidic to neutral soil. In alkaline soils it may develop nutrient deficiencies. The plant does not tolerate drought and needs regular water and fertilizer. Its salt tolerance is low. Diseases and pest problems are insignificant.

Recommended uses: This palm is a conversation piece. Make it a focal point; plant it alone where you can appreciate its unusual form.

Traveler's palm

Washingtonia filifera
wash-ing-TOH-nee-uh fil-IF-er-uh
Desert fan palm

- **Size:** 50–70'H×10–12'W
- **Light:** Full sun
- **Water:** Drought tolerant
- **Minimum temperature:** 22°F
- **Features:** Single-trunk fan-leaf palm with khaki green leaves

Desert fan palm

Desert fan palm is an impressive native of the American Southwest where it grows in the desert near water sources. The trunk can be 3 feet in diameter and, unless trimmed, is covered with a petticoat of old leaves except in its oldest part. The 3- to 4-foot-wide leaves are khaki green with whitish threads between the segments, and each leaf develops droopy segment tips. The leaf stems are armed with sharp teeth. The small fruit is brownish black.

Care: Well-drained acidic or alkaline soil suits desert fan palm. It is a drought-tolerant palm best adapted to dry climates. Rachis blight can be a serious problem. Nutrient deficiencies are rare. The plant's salt tolerance is fair.

Recommended uses: Desert fan palm has an imposing presence that is out of scale in small landscapes. It makes an excellent street tree and works well in formal situations. A grouping of varied heights is especially impressive.

Washingtonia robusta
wash-ing-TOH-nee-uh roh-BUST-uh
Mexican fan palm

- **Size:** 60–80'H×8–10'W
- **Light:** Full sun
- **Water:** Drought tolerant to low
- **Minimum temperature:** 25°F
- **Features:** Single-trunk fan-leaf palm with bright green leaves

Mexican fan palm

This native of Mexico has a growth habit similar to that of desert fan palm. It grows taller and has an 18-inch-thick trunk covered in reddish brown leaf bases if the petticoat of old leaves remains intact. The 3- to 4-foot-wide leaves are deep emerald green and rest on shorter armed leaf stems than those of its cousin. Its tiny fruits are brownish black.

Care: Mexican fan palm does well in well-drained acidic or alkaline soil. The plant grows quickly when given regular water and fertilizer. It tolerates short drought periods. Its salt tolerance is good. Disease and pest problems do not become serious, and nutrient deficiencies are rare.

Recommended uses: This palm looks best when planted in a grouping rather than as an individual. It makes an excellent street tree. Because of its height it looks great around tall homes, where it softens hard architectural lines. It is also attractive in planting beds with other foliage plants.

Wodyetia bifurcata
wod-YET-ee-uh by-foor-KAHT-uh
Foxtail palm

- **Size:** 40–50'H×10–12'W
- **Light:** Full sun
- **Water:** Drought tolerant to low
- **Minimum temperature:** 30°F
- **Features:** Single-trunk feather-leaf palm with crownshaft

Native to far northern Queensland, Australia, and discovered only in the early 1980s, foxtail palm has already become widely cultivated. The plant may develop a bulge midway up its smooth light gray trunk that otherwise is 8 to 10 inches thick. The crownshaft is lighter green than the dark green 7- to 9-foot-long leaves. Narrow leaflets radiate in all directions from the leaf stem, giving the leaf an extremely feathery look. The fruit is brilliant red when ripe.

Care: Moderately fast-growing foxtail palm requires well-drained acidic soil. It develops nutrient deficiencies in alkaline conditions. Regular water and fertilizer are essential for strong growth. The plant has fair salt tolerance. It has no major disease or pest problems.

Recommended uses: A single foxtail palm is nice, but it looks best in a grouping. It's superb with a groundcover or other large-leaf foliage plants such as philodendron and elephant's ear beneath it. This palm also makes an elegant street tree.

Foxtail palm

Zombia antillarum
ZAHM-bee-uh an-til-LAR-um
Zombie palm

- **Size:** 12–15'H×8–12'W
- **Light:** Full sun
- **Water:** Drought tolerant to low
- **Minimum temperature:** 30°F
- **Features:** Multitrunk fan-leaf palm with spiny fibers on trunk

Zombie palm

The 3- to 4-inch-thick trunks of this Hispaniola native are covered in coarse fibers and spines from old leaf bases, creating an intricate design. The 3-foot-wide leaves are medium to deep green and shiny. The marble-size fruit becomes whitish when ripe.

Care: Zombie palm prefers alkaline soil but tolerates slightly acidic soil as long as the drainage is good. It thrives on regular water and fertilizer. The plant does not tolerate drought well and has fair salt tolerance. It needs full sun to do well; in shade it stretches and loses its compact form. Insect pests and diseases are seldom a major problem.

Recommended uses: Because zombie palm is a dense clumper, it can be used as a screening plant. But because it is a slow grower you'll need patience until it gets tall enough to block a view. Its major appeal is as an intimate focal point featuring the intricate detail of its trunks.

PALMLIKE PLANTS

Just when you think you know palms, imposters arrive on the scene to confound the situation. To add to the confusion, some such as king sago palm, queen sago palm, cardboard palm, Madagascar palm, screw palm, palm grass, and ponytail palm have common names that include the word "palm."

In this section you'll learn about these palm imposters. All of these palmlike plants complement actual palms in the landscape and are frequently used side by side with them. The plant descriptions here include the same categories of information used in the palm gallery to help you determine which plants to choose and where best to use them in your landscape.

Most palms develop a trunk with an arching spray of leaves on top. People often think that any plant exhibiting such an appearance must be a palm. However, many plants that grow in a similar form belong to other plant families. Palmlike plants may belong to the following families and differ from palms in the ways described.

Cycads Prehistoric seed-bearing plants that have been around for 230 million years, cycads are more closely related to pine trees than to palms. Separate male and female plants produce cones similar to those of pines. All are heavily endangered plants in their native habitats. Many palm enthusiasts are also cycad enthusiasts, probably because cycads look so much like palms.

Tree ferns Although tree ferns resemble fishtail palms in their leaves and overall appearance, they are true ferns that reproduce by spores instead of seeds. They have existed on the planet even longer than cycads.

Succulents Dracaenas, ponytail palm, and yuccas are all closely related to agaves, but because of their growth habit they are sometimes mistaken for palms—although they have different leaves (theirs are straplike), flowers, and seeds than palms.

Other palmlike plants Madagascar palm resembles succulents, but it belongs to the same family as oleander and frangipani. Screw pine has its own family, and traveler's palm (*Ravenala madagascariensis*) belongs to the bird-of-paradise family. All are very different from palms even if they resemble them in a superficial way. Panama hat plant and palm grass are monocots like palms but differ enough to be classified into different families.

The following pages list only 27 common palm imposters. Considering that the cycad family alone contains 200 species, this list is only a sampling. However, it will help you to distinguish palmlike plants from palms and provide information on how to grow them.

▼ **Cycads closely resemble palms but are not closely related to them. Many grow in a clump with no trunk until they become old.**

PALMLIKE PLANT GALLERY

Angiopteris evecta
an-jee-AHP-ter-iss ee-VEK-tuh

King fern

- **Size:** 12–15'H×12–15'W
- **Light:** Moderate shade
- **Water:** Moderate
- **Minimum temperature:** 32°F
- **Features:** Single-trunk bipinnate-leaf fern with fibrous base

King fern

King fern is native to Australia, New Guinea, and Malaysia. It has a short thick trunk to 3 feet tall and 2 feet thick. Its leaves are similar to the large triangular ones of giant solitaire palm. Under ideal conditions the stiffly upright dark green leaves can grow 15 feet or longer. The plant reproduces by spores, which develop on the undersides of older leaves.
Care: This moderately fast-growing fern likes humusy acidic to alkaline soil. It needs plentiful water and cannot tolerate drying out. It has no salt tolerance. Nutrient deficiencies are rare if the plant is fed regularly. Diseases and insect pests pose no serious problem.
Recommended uses: A large fern like this needs ample space to grow. A low groundcover planted underneath is fine, but to make this fern a focal point keep larger plants away from it.

Beaucarnea recurvata
bo-KAR-nee-uh reh-koor-VAYT-uh

Ponytail palm

- **Size:** 12–20'H×6–12'W
- **Light:** Full sun
- **Water:** Drought tolerant
- **Minimum temperature:** 28°F
- **Features:** Single-trunk tree with swollen base

Ponytail palm is an agave relative native to Mexico, where it can reach 30 feet tall. Its trunk is distinguished by a swollen base, which can reach 6 feet across in old plants. The trunk may or may not branch. The long, thin medium green to olive green leaves grow up to 6 feet long. This plant develops seeds in winged capsules. It is sometimes classified as *Nolina recurvata*.
Care: Well-drained sandy soil is ideal and it can be either acidic or alkaline. Slow-growing ponytail palm thrives on light watering and regular feeding. Its drought tolerance is excellent but its salt tolerance is only fair. The plant has few disease, insect pest, or nutrient problems.
Recommended uses: Ponytail palm adds a great sculptural quality to the garden, so be sure to locate it where you can view its entire form from top to bottom. It also looks striking planted with other low-water-use plants such as cactus, succulents, and cycads. Ponytail palm is an excellent easy-care indoor plant.

Ponytail palm

Blechnum gibbum
BLEK-num GIB-um

Dwarf tree fern

- **Size:** 3–4'H×3–4'W
- **Light:** Moderate shade
- **Water:** Moderate
- **Minimum temperature:** 30°F
- **Features:** Single-trunk feather-leaf fern with fibrous trunk

Dwarf tree fern

Dwarf tree fern is native to islands of the South Pacific. It is relatively small but looks deceptively palmlike. The fibrous trunk is only about 2 inches thick and with age grows to only about 3 or 4 feet high. The 2- to 3-foot-long leaves are light grassy green. The plant reproduces through spores, which develop on undersides of older leaves.
Care: Dwarf tree fern, which grows at a moderate rate, prefers humusy acidic to alkaline soil. It cannot tolerate dry periods; water it often and regularly. The plant is not salt-tolerant. Avoid nutrient deficiencies with regular feeding. Diseases and insect problems are rare.
Recommended uses: Dwarf tree fern is a delightful small accent plant for intimate shady spots where you can appreciate it at close range. Contrast its light green leaves with darker surrounding foliage. In a larger space a grouping of several dwarf tree ferns is effective.

Carludovica palmata
kar-loo-DOH-vih-kuh palm-AYT-uh

Panama hat plant

- **Size:** 6–8'H×4–6'W
- **Light:** Moderate shade
- **Water:** Moderate
- **Minimum temperature:** 32°F
- **Features:** Multishoot fan-leaf plant with no trunk

Panama hat plant

Panama hat plant looks so much like a palm that it is easily mistaken for one. This native of Central and South American rain forests is trunkless, its fan-shape leaves arising from the ground on long leaf stems. In Ecuador the 2- to 4-foot-wide deep green leaves are used to make fine-quality hats. Panama hat plant sends up a spathe (flower bract) from the base of leaves and produces an orange to red fruit.
Care: This fast grower does well in humusy acidic to alkaline soil. It thrives on constant moisture (don't let it dry out) and regular fertilizer. The plant has little salt tolerance. Nutrient, disease, and pest problems seldom occur.
Recommended uses: Panama hat plant has what it takes to be the centerpiece in a rain forest-style garden. It is especially appealing when partnered with contrasting foliage under a high canopy.

Ceratozamia robusta
seh-ray-toh-ZAY-mee-uh roh-BUST-uh

Imperial palm, Forest pineapple

- **Size:** 10–12'H×10–12'W
- **Light:** Moderate to light shade
- **Water:** Drought tolerant
- **Minimum temperature:** 30°F
- **Features:** Single-trunk feather-leaf cycad with a short trunk

Native to Mexico, Belize, and Guatemala this plant develops a short, wide trunk with age, and it rarely branches. The 12-foot-long leaves are glossy deep green. When they newly emerge the leaves are usually rusty red and are held upright. The leaf stems are armed with prickles. Off-white seeds drop from the cone when they ripen.
Care: This moderately fast grower prefers well-drained sandy soil, which can be either acidic or alkaline. It tolerates short dry periods but thrives on regular water and fertilizer. The plant has only slight salt tolerance. Although this cycad tolerates full sun, it looks much better in some shade. It has no major nutrient or disease problems but occasionally develops scale insect infestations.
Recommended uses: At home in an understory mix of foliage plants and palms, this cycad is an attractive accent plant that is especially showy when its new flush of reddish leaves emerges. Repeated plantings of groups are also quite appealing.

Imperial palm

Curculigo capitulata
koor-KYOO-lih-go kuh-pit-yoo-LAYT-uh

Palm grass

- **Size:** 3–5'H×1–2'W
- **Light:** Moderate to light shade
- **Water:** Moderate
- **Minimum temperature:** 30°F
- **Features:** Spreading groundcover

Palm grass

From Southeast Asia and Australia, palm grass multiplies readily by rhizomes (horizontally spreading underground stems). Its leaves look like those of palm seedlings and are the source of its common name. Clusters of yellow flowers form at the base of the plant in summer.
Care: This moderately fast-growing member of the amaryllis family likes acidic to neutral soil with some organic matter mixed in. Palm grass thrives on regular water and fertilizer. It has no drought or salt tolerance. The plant is unaffected by diseases and insect pests. It yellows in full sun and needs some shade to look its best.
Recommended uses: Palm grass makes a wonderful tall groundcover along pathways or mixed with ferns and flowering plants. It is excellent in understory plantings that mimic a rain forest.

Cyathea cooperi
sy-AY-thee-uh KOOP-er-eye
Australian tree fern

- **Size: 12–20'H×10–15'W**
- **Light: Light shade**
- **Water: Moderate**
- **Minimum temperature: 28°F**
- **Features: Single-trunk, bipinnate-leaf fern with fibrous trunk**

Australian tree fern

This tree fern reaches a height of 40 feet or more in its native Australia. The 3- to 6-inch thick tannish brown trunk is usually covered in fibers that assist in water uptake. The 6- to 10-foot-long triangular leaves, which are light to medium green, are similar to those of fishtail palms. The plant reproduces by spores, which develop on the undersides of older leaves.

Care: A humusy acidic to slightly alkaline soil is ideal. The plant needs regular water; it cannot tolerate drying out. This fast grower thrives on regular fertilizer and rarely has nutrient deficiencies. Diseases and pest problems are rare. The plant has no salt tolerance.

Recommended uses: A grouping of Australian tree ferns under a high canopy creates a magnificent lacy secondary canopy that can shield smaller foliage plants. Even though it takes several years to get big enough to form that lower canopy it's still very attractive.

Cycas revoluta
SY-kus rev-oh-LOOT-uh
King sago palm

- **Size: 4–8'H×4–8'W**
- **Light: Full sun**
- **Water: Drought tolerant**
- **Minimum temperature: 15°F**
- **Features: Single-trunk feather-leaf cycad that branches**

Native to Ryukyu and Kyushu islands of Japan, king sago palm has a brownish black trunk generally 12 to 18 inches thick. The 2- to 4-foot-long deep dark green leaves are quite stiff. Orangish red seeds fall from the cone when they mature.

Care: Slow-growing king sago palm prefers well-drained sandy soil, which can be either acidic or alkaline—though in alkaline soils it can develop a manganese deficiency if it is not fed regularly. The plant is very drought-tolerant, but likes regular water. Its salt tolerance is good. All cycads, including king sago palm, are highly susceptible to the potentially devastating Asian cycad scale.

Recommended uses: Long used as an ornamental plant throughout the world, king sago palm is eye-catching as a specimen in an open space or in a grouping with other foliage plants. It is superb as a container plant for pool or patio areas and also holds up well indoors.

King sago palm and cone (inset)

Cycas rumphii
SY-kus RUM-fee-eye
Queen sago palm

- **Size: 10–15'H×8–12'W**
- **Light: Full sun**
- **Water: Low**
- **Minimum temperature: 28°F**
- **Features: Single-trunk feather-leaf cycad that branches**

Queen sago palm

Widespread throughout Southeast Asia and the South Pacific, this species is often confused with *C. circinalis*, an Indian native. The trunk of queen sago palm is 12 to 18 inches in diameter and swollen at the base. Male plants in particular branch from the upper trunk or base. The 6- to 8-foot-long leaves are deep green. Orange seeds fall from the cone when they ripen.

Care: Queen sago palm likes acidic or alkaline sandy soil that drains well. Regular water and fertilizer will keep this cycad growing at a moderate rate. It withstands brief dry periods, and it is not very salt-tolerant. Diseases and nutrient deficiencies are seldom a concern, but the plant is susceptible to the Asian cycad scale, which is difficult to control once an infestation becomes established.

Recommended uses: Queen sago will become a focal point in any garden. It is a gorgeous plant on its own in an open space or with low-growing plants beneath it.

Dioon edule
dy-OON ED-yoo-lee
Virgin palm

- **Size: 6–10'H×5–15'W**
- **Light: Full sun**
- **Water: Drought tolerant**
- **Minimum temperature: 22°F**
- **Features: Single-trunk feather-leaf cycad that branches**

Virgin palm

Several forms of this Mexican native exist, each with a slightly different appearance and color. The width of the plant depends on the amount of branching that it develops. Trunks form with great age and can be 8 to 16 inches thick. The 3- to 5-foot-long leaves range from light grassy green to deep bluish green. The seeds are yellow when mature.
Care: This slow grower does well in either acidic or alkaline soil as long as it drains well. Virgin palm is very drought-tolerant but likes to be watered and fed regularly. Nutritional deficiencies, diseases, and insect pests are rare. The plant has good salt tolerance.
Recommended uses: Virgin palm is an exquisite accent plant even when small. It is all the more attractive in a grouping surrounded by a low groundcover or mulch. Combine it with giant dioon or other cycads to create a

Dioon spinulosum
dy-OON spin-yoo-LO-sum
Giant dioon

- **Size: 12–20'H×8–12'W**
- **Light: Light shade to full sun**
- **Water: Drought tolerant**
- **Minimum temperature: 28°F**
- **Features: Single-trunk feather-leaf cycad with spiny leaves**

Giant dioon is a Mexican native with an 8- to 10-inch-diameter trunk that bulges at the base. The beautifully arching leaves are medium green and 5 to 7 feet long in full sun; they are deep green and can be longer in shade. The leaflets are armed with small teeth or spines along their edges. The mature cone breaks apart releasing brown seeds.
Care: A moderate grower, this cycad succeeds in either acidic or alkaline well-drained soil. It thrives on regular light watering and regular feeding. It tolerates short dry periods well, and its salt tolerance is fair. The plant has no serious nutrient, disease, or insect pest problems.
Recommended uses: Giant dioon is a graceful beauty in the landscape all by itself, but it also is attractive in a grouping and is an essential component of a cycad garden. It works just as well with other foliage plants in a rain forest-style planting. Keep it away from walkways where its spiny leaves can inflict harm to passersby.

Giant dioon

Dracaena arborea
druh-SEEN-uh ar-BOR-ee-uh
Tree dracaena

- **Size: 12–15'H×5–8'W**
- **Light: Full sun**
- **Water: Drought tolerant**
- **Minimum temperature: 30°F**
- **Features: Single-trunk branching tree**

Tree dracaena

This native of tropical Africa has a grayish trunk that forks readily into 3- to 4-inch-diameter branches. The top of each branch develops a crown with many narrow straplike leaves, each 2 to 3 feet long and deep green. Whitish flowers are followed by red fruit.
Care: A slow to moderate grower, tree dracaena requires well-drained soil that can be either acidic or alkaline. Although drought-tolerant, it appreciates occasional water. Regular feeding prevents any nutrient deficiencies. The plant is quite salt-tolerant and has few disease or insect pest problems.
Recommended uses: Tree dracaena is striking with other drought-tolerant plants such as cactus, succulents, and cycads and is also attractive combined with broadleaf foliage plants. Its dark green foliage contrasts beautifully with silvery or bluish green drought-tolerant plants.

Dracaena draco
druh-SEEN-uh DRAY-ko

Dragontree

- **Size:** 15–25'H×15–25'W
- **Light:** Full sun
- **Water:** Drought tolerant
- **Minimum temperature:** 28°F
- **Features:** Single-trunk, branching tree

Dragontree

Native to the Canary Islands, dragontree is cultivated throughout the Mediterranean region, in California, and in other areas with a similar dry-summer climate. The main trunk is gray and grows 2 feet or more in diameter. It branches heavily to form an umbrella shape, and a crown of straplike grayish green leaves to 3 feet long develops at the end of each branch. Creamy white flowers are followed by orange fruit.

Care: This plant needs well-drained soil, which can be acidic or alkaline. Keep the plant on the dry side—water it minimally and only during long dry spells. Light feeding is sufficient for this very slow grower. Its salt tolerance is good, and any problems with insect pests, diseases, or nutrition are minimal.

Recommended uses: Dragontree is an excellent plant for a low-water garden. Although you'll have to wait many years for the characteristic umbrella shape to develop, your patience will be rewarded with a dramatic specimen plant.

Dracaena marginata
druh-SEEN-uh mar-jin-AYT-uh

Red-edge dracaena, Madagascar dragontree

- **Size:** 10–15'H×6–10'W
- **Light:** Light shade to full sun
- **Water:** Moderate
- **Minimum temperature:** 30°F
- **Features:** Single-trunk, branching tree

This Madagascar native has a wild, sculptural appearance with branches that go off in all directions. The main trunk can grow to 8 inches or more in diameter, but the branches are less than 2 inches thick. Clustered at the branch ends are straplike leaves less than 2 feet long; they are dark green with a narrow red border. The fruit is orange.

Care: A slow to moderate grower, red-edge dracaena succeeds in acidic or alkaline soil that drains well. It needs regular water and fertilizer for strong growth. The plant tolerates brief dry periods once established and has fair salt tolerance. Diseases and nutritional deficiencies are infrequent. Spider mites sometimes attack the plant when it is grown indoors.

Recommended uses: Red-edge dracaena has long been cultivated throughout the world as both a landscape and container plant. In the landscape it looks best planted against a wall where its unusual form can best be appreciated. It is an excellent container plant for the patio or indoors.

Red-edge dracaena

Encephalartos ferox
en-sef-uh-LAR-tos FEHR-ahx

Zululand cycad

- **Size:** 4–7'H×5–9'W
- **Light:** Light shade to full sun
- **Water:** Drought tolerant
- **Minimum temperature:** 28°F
- **Features:** Single-trunk feather-leaf cycad

Zululand cycad

This native of South Africa seldom has an aboveground trunk. The 3- to 6-foot-long glossy deep green leaves vary in shape from curly to flat. They are stiff and armed with teeth on their edges. The orangish red cones contrast beautifully with the foliage. Red seeds fall from the cones when they ripen.

Care: Slow-growing Zululand cycad likes well-drained sandy soil that is alkaline to slightly acidic. It only needs regular light watering and regular feeding for optimum growth. It has some drought tolerance and good salt tolerance. The plant occasionally becomes infested with scale insects but it has no major disease or nutrient problems.

Recommended uses: This extremely ornamental cycad looks best under a high canopy, though it becomes a focal point wherever it is planted.

Encephalartos gratus
en-sef-uh-LAHR-tos GRAT-us

Mulanje cycad

- **Size: 8–12'H×8–10'W**
- **Light: Light shade to full sun**
- **Water: Low**
- **Minimum temperature: 30°F**
- **Features: Single-trunk feather-leaf cycad**

Mulanje cycad

A stocky trunk to 2 feet thick is characteristic of this South African native. The shiny medium to dark green leaves up to 7 feet long arch gracefully, especially in shade. The leaflets have a few small teeth along their edges. The mature cones break apart to reveal orangish red seeds.
Care: This plant grows in acidic or alkaline soil that drains well. Though it tolerates brief dry periods well, it appreciates regular water and fertilizer. Its salt tolerance is slight. Scale insects and sooty mold occasionally affect the plant. It has no major disease or nutritional problems.
Recommended uses: This cycad is a gorgeous addition to the landscape planted by itself. It also looks good grouped in an open area or grown with other plants under a high canopy.

Encephalartos lehmannii
en-sef-uh-LAHR-tos lay-MAHN-ee-eye

Karoo cycad

- **Size: 4–6'H×3–5'W**
- **Light: Full sun**
- **Water: Drought tolerant**
- **Minimum temperature: 25°F**
- **Features: Multitrunk feather-leaf cycad with bluish leaves**

Native to South Africa, this extremely attractive cycad develops short trunks with age that can become 18 inches thick. The 3- to 4-foot-long upright leaves are covered in silvery blue wax, giving them a bluish green or silvery blue color. The stiff leaflets are often sparsely armed with spines on their edges. Red seeds fall from the cone when they ripen.
Care: Very slow-growing karoo cycad requires well-drained alkaline to slightly acidic soil. This cycad rarely needs any additional watering. Water it only during extended drought. It seldom develops nutrient deficiencies if it is fed regularly. The plant has excellent drought and salt tolerance. Diseases and insect pests are rare.
Recommended uses: This cycad is a striking accent plant whether planted alone or grouped. It looks natural planted in a rock garden among cactus and succulents.

Karoo cycad

Lepidozamia hopei
lep-ih-doh-ZAY-mee-uh HOHP-ee-eye

Wunu

- **Size: 15–20'H×12–18'W**
- **Light: Moderate to light shade**
- **Water: Drought tolerant**
- **Minimum temperature: 30°F**
- **Features: Single-trunk feather-leaf cycad that sometimes branches**

Wunu

This is the tallest-growing cycad, and in its native habitat in Queensland, Australia, ancient plants may reach 55 feet tall, though in gardens it won't grow nearly that tall. The trunk is about 12 inches wide with a much thicker base. The 6- to 10-foot-long leaves are glossy medium to dark green. Red seeds fall from the cone when they mature.
Care: Well-drained acidic or alkaline soil suits this slow grower. It appreciates light watering and regular feeding. The plant tolerates short dry periods and has slight salt tolerance. It has no major disease, insect pest, or nutrient problems.
Recommended uses: An ideal location for this cycad is under a high canopy of trees with contrasting foliage around it. Its tropical look works well in a rain forest-style garden.

Macrozamia communis
mak-ro-ZAYM-ee-uh kah-MYOO-niss

Burrawong

- **Size:** 5–7'H×7–9'W
- **Light:** Light shade
- **Water:** Drought tolerant
- **Minimum temperature:** 25°F
- **Features:** Feather-leaf cycad with underground trunk

Burrawong

This cycad comes from coastal New South Wales, Australia, where it grows under eucalyptus trees. It rarely has an aboveground trunk and tends to be unbranched. The deep emerald green feathery leaves—often more than 50 in the crown— arch gracefully. Scarlet seeds fall from the cone when they ripen.

Care: Burrawong prefers cool nights. It tolerates the heat of South Florida, but does better in California, Central Florida, and points farther north where it is hardy. It needs well-drained acidic or alkaline soil. This slow grower needs regular water and fertilizer. The plant has slight drought tolerance. Scale insects can be an occasional problem. Nutrient deficiencies and disease problems are rare.

Recommended uses: A delightful accent under a high canopy tree, burrawong looks good in groups and needs no other plants to complement it.

Microcycas calocoma
my-kro-SY-kus kal-o-KO-muh

Cork palm

- **Size:** 12–15'H×5–7'W
- **Light:** Light shade to full sun
- **Water:** Drought tolerant
- **Minimum temperature:** 28°F
- **Features:** Single-trunk feather-leaf cycad that sometimes branches

An endangered cycad from the mountains of western Cuba where it can grow more than 30 feet tall this cycad has a dark brown trunk up to 2 feet thick at the base. The 2- to 4-foot-long medium to dark green leaves are made up of leaflets that angle down from the leaf stem in a V shape. Pinkish red seeds are mature when the cone disintegrates.

Care: This slow grower needs well-drained sandy soil that is alkaline to neutral. It is drought-tolerant but responds favorably to light watering and regular feeding. Its salt tolerance is fair. The plant has few nutrient, insect pest, and disease problems, although scale insects and sooty mold occasionally occur.

Recommended uses: Cork palm is rare in cultivation. Search it out for an absolutely gorgeous addition to the landscape. Show it off as a focal point either alone or with other contrasting foliage around it.

Cork palm

Pachypodium geayi
pak-ih-PO-dee-um GAY-ee

Madagascar palm

- **Size:** 10–15'H×3–4'W
- **Light:** Full sun
- **Water:** Drought tolerant
- **Minimum temperature:** 30°F
- **Features:** Single-trunk succulent shrub with spiny trunk

Madagascar palm

This relative of oleander and frangipani from Madagascar is a succulent shrub that branches with age. The light gray trunk is covered in spines. The narrow leaves, growing 12 to 18 inches long, are shiny grayish green. The plant takes many years to reach maturity but in time develops clusters of attractive white flowers.

Care: Slow-growing Madagascar palm prefers a very porous soil, which can be acidic or alkaline. The plant is drought-tolerant but likes light watering and regular feeding. It will rot at its base and die if kept too wet. Its salt tolerance is good. Nutritional deficiencies, diseases, and insect pests are rare.

Recommended uses: Madagascar palm combines well with other succulents and cactus in a low-water-use landscape. It looks natural planted among boulders in a rock garden. Its unusual form makes an excellent focal point.

Pachypodium rutenbergianum
pak-ih-PO-dee-um root-en-bur-gee-AHN-um

Madagascar palm

- **Size:** 10–15'H×6–10'W
- **Light:** Full sun
- **Water:** Drought tolerant
- **Minimum temperature:** 32°F
- **Features:** Single-trunk treelike succulent with spiny trunk

Madagascar palm

This Madagascar native, which shares its common name with *P. geayi*, also has a light gray trunk with short spines. But this species branches readily, forming a small tree. A crown of narrow bright green leaves 10 to 12 inches long develops at the end of each branch. The plant is deciduous in winter and bears white flowers with pale yellow centers in very early spring.

Care: Madagascar palm must have well-drained soil, which can be either acidic or alkaline. It grows at a moderate rate and thrives on light watering and regular feeding. It has no major nutritional, disease, or pest problems.

Recommended uses: Partner this plant with cactus and succulents in a low-water-use landscape. It provides some shade for smaller drought-tolerant plants that need less sun.

Pandanus utilis
pan-DAN-us YOO-til-iss

Screw pine, Screw palm

- **Size:** 20–25'H×15–20'W
- **Light:** Full sun
- **Water:** Drought tolerant to low
- **Minimum temperature:** 30°F
- **Features:** Single-trunk tree with serrated leaves

Screw pine, also called screw palm, is neither a pine nor a palm, but rather in a family of its own. It has been so widely cultivated that its exact origin is unknown, but Madagascar is the likely source. The gray trunk forms stilt roots (aboveground brace roots) up to 6 feet above the soil. The plant's spreading branches give it a treelike appearance. The 6-foot-long, narrow, serrated, deep green leaves are arranged in a spiral pattern. Fruit that looks like a hand grenade is borne in clusters.

Care: This moderate grower does well in acidic or alkaline soil containing some organic matter. It needs regular water and feeding. Nutritional deficiencies, diseases, and pest problems are rare. Its salt tolerance is good and its drought tolerance is slight.

Recommended uses: A good focal point in the landscape, screw pine is most striking when located by itself where you can see its full form from top to bottom. It also grows well as a houseplant in bright locations. The serrated leaf edges can inflict painful wounds, so place screw pine out of the line of pedestrian traffic.

Screw pine

Ravenala madagascariensis
rav-eh-NAL-uh mad-uh-gas-kar-ee-EN-sis

Traveler's palm

- **Size:** 25–35'H×12–20'W
- **Light:** Full sun
- **Water:** Drought tolerant to low
- **Minimum temperature:** 30°F
- **Features:** Multitrunk fan-shape tree

Traveler's palm

This native of Madagascar and relative of bird-of-paradise can be massive with a trunk 2 feet thick. Its gracefully arched leaves are arranged in a single plane creating the appearance of a giant fan. The 10-to 12-foot-long deep green leaves are smooth edged until the wind causes them to split. Green bird-of-paradise flower bracts conceal small white flowers that develop blue seeds when mature.

Care: Traveler's palm is not particular about whether the soil is acidic or alkaline as long as it contains some organic matter. The plant is a strong grower that needs regular water and fertilizer. It has little drought tolerance and fair salt tolerance. Pests, diseases, and nutrient problems are rare.

Recommended uses: This is a huge plant that should be viewed from a distance. It looks best when surrounded by open space or as a towering background specimen. It makes a great conversation piece.

Yucca rigida
YUK-uh RIJ-ih-duh

Blue yucca

- **Size:** 10–15'H×3–5'W
- **Light:** Full sun
- **Water:** Drought tolerant
- **Minimum temperature:** 15°F
- **Features:** Single-trunk treelike succulent

Blue yucca

Blue yucca is a sparsely branched native of northwestern Mexico. The 3- to 4-inch-thick trunk is usually covered in a sheath of old leaves. The silvery blue leaves are arranged in a rounded crown atop the stem. Each leaf is 2 to 3 feet long with a sharp, pointed leaf tip. The creamy white flower cluster rises straight up from the top of the leaf crown.

Care: Slow-growing blue yucca needs well-drained soil but is not particular about whether it is acidic or alkaline. It needs no additional water once established but appreciates watering during extreme drought. It does not do well in a wet climate or heavy soil. With regular feeding, nutrient deficiencies are rare. It has no major disease or pest problems, and its salt tolerance is good.

Recommended uses: A wonderful accent plant, blue yucca is an ideal companion for other succulents and cactus in a low-water use garden.

Zamia furfuracea
ZAYM-ee-uh fur-fyoo-RAY-see-uh

Cardboard zamia, Cardboard palm

- **Size:** 4–5'H×5–7'W
- **Light:** Light shade to full sun
- **Water:** Drought tolerant
- **Minimum temperature:** 28°F
- **Features:** Multitrunk feather-leaf cycad

This Mexican native develops a tight clump of leaf crowns on an underground stem. The 2- to 4-foot long (longer in shade) leaves are dark olive green, sometimes with a brownish green underside; the new leaves emerge bright yellowish green. The leaflet shapes vary but they are always thick and do not bend easily—just like cardboard. Red seeds drop from the cones when ripe.

Care: Slow-growing cardboard zamia prefers well-drained sandy soil that is alkaline to slightly acidic. It thrives on light watering and feeding. Its tolerance to drought and salt are good. Scale insects and sooty mold may develop, but otherwise the plant has few nutrient or pest problems.

Recommended uses: This cycad is a striking small accent plant. It also can be planted in clusters as a large groundcover plant. The leaves stretch in shade, giving the plant a graceful look.

Cardboard zamia

Zamia pumila
ZAYM-ee-uh POO-mil-uh

Coontie

- **Size:** 2–4'H×3–5'W
- **Light:** Light shade to full sun
- **Water:** Drought tolerant
- **Minimum temperature:** 22°F
- **Features:** Multitrunk feather-leaf cycad

Coontie

Native to Florida, Georgia, and the West Indies, coontie is a trunkless cycad that creates tightly clumped clusters of leaves as it ages. The shiny grassy green to dark green leaves vary in length from 12 to 24 inches; they also vary in width. Its color is more intense in shade. Red seeds drop from the cones when they are mature. It is sometimes classified as *Z. integrifolia*.

Care: Slow-growing coontie does well in well-drained sandy soil that is alkaline to slightly acidic. Although this cycad is drought-tolerant, it likes light watering and regular feeding. Its salt tolerance is excellent. Scale insects and sooty mold are occasional problems. Nutritional and disease problems are rare.

Recommended uses: A group of coonties makes an excellent groundcover in a planting bed. It also makes a good small focal point when it grows larger.

RESOURCES

Societies

The International Palm Society
P. O. Box 1897
Lawrence, KS 66044-8897 USA
www.palms.org

**The Palm and Cycad Societies
   of Australia**
P.O. Box 1134
Milton, Queensland 4064 Australia
07/3255-8088
www.pacsoa.org.au

Palm and Cycad Society of Florida
www.plantapalm.com

Public gardens with extensive palm collections

Balboa Park
1549 El Prado
San Diego, CA 92101
619/239-0512
www.balboapark.org

Fairchild Tropical Botanical Garden
10901 Old Cutler Road
Coral Gables, FL 33156
305/667-1651
www.fairchildgarden.org

Flamingo Gardens
3750 S. Flamingo Road
Davie, FL 33330
954/473-2955
www.flamingogardens.org

Foster Botanical Garden
50 N. Vineyard Boulevard
Honolulu, HI 96817
808/522-7066
www.honolulu.gov/parks/hbg/fbg.htm

Gizella Kopsick Palm Arboretum
North Shore Drive at 10th Ave. NE
St. Petersburg Parks Dept.
1400 19th St. N
St. Petersburg, FL 33713
727/893-7335
http://cms.stpete.org/default.
   asp?page=1460

Harold L. Lyon Arboretum
University of Hawaii-Manoa
3860 Manoa Road
Honolulu, HI, 96822
808/988-0456
www.hawaii.edu/lyonarboretum

Ho'omaluhia Botanical Garden
45-680 Luluku Road
Kaneohe, HI 96744
808/233-7323
www.honolulu.gov/parks/hbg/hmbg.htm

Huntington Botanical Garden
1151 Oxford Road
San Marino, CA 91108
626/405-2100
www.huntington.org

Lakeside Palmetum
666 Bellevue Avenue
Oakland, CA 94610
www.palmsnc.org/pages/palmetum.php

Montgomery Botanical Center
open by appointment only
11901 Old Cutler Road
Coral Gables, FL 33156
305/667-3800
www.montgomerybotanical.org

National Tropical Botanical Garden
3530 Papalina Road
Kalaheo, HI 96741
808/332-7324
www.ntbg.org

Pana'ewa Rainforest Zoo and Gardens
Hwy. 11
Hilo, Hawaii
P.O. Box 738
Kea'au, HI 96749
808/959-9233
www.hilozoo.com

Quail Botanical Garden
230 Encinitas Drive
Encinitas, CA 92024
760/436-3036
www.qbgardens.org

**The University of California Botanical
   Garden**
200 Centennial Drive
Berkeley, CA 94720-5045
510/643-2755
http://Botanicalgarden.berkeley.edu

Waimea Valley Audubon Center
59-864 Kamehameha Hwy.
Haleiwa, HI 96712
808/638-9199
http://waimea.audubon.org

INDEX

Note: Page references in **bold type** refer to Gallery entries and include photographs. Page references in *italic type* refer to additional photographs, illustrations, and information in captions. Plants are listed by their common names.

METRIC CONVERSIONS

U.S. UNITS TO METRIC EQUIVALENTS			METRIC EQUIVALENTS TO U.S. UNITS		
To Convert From	**Multiply by**	**To Get**	**To Convert From**	**Multiply by**	**To Get**
Inches	25.4	Millimeters	Millimeters	0.0394	Inches
Inches	2.54	Centimeters	Centimeters	0.3937	Inches
Feet	30.48	Centimeters	Centimeters	0.0328	Feet
Feet	0.3048	Meters	Meters	3.2808	Feet
Yards	0.9144	Meters	Meters	1.0936	Yards
Square inches	6.4516	Square centimeters	Square centimeters	0.1550	Square inches
Square feet	0.0929	Square meters	Square meters	10.764	Square feet
Square yards	0.8361	Square meters	Square meters	1.1960	Square yards
Acres	0.4047	Hectares	Hectares	2.4711	Acres
Cubic inches	16.387	Cubic centimeters	Cubic centimeters	0.0610	Cubic inches
Cubic feet	0.0283	Cubic meters	Cubic meters	35.315	Cubic feet
Cubic feet	28.316	Liters	Liters	0.0353	Cubic feet
Cubic yards	0.7646	Cubic meters	Cubic meters	1.308	Cubic yards
Cubic yards	764.55	Liters	Liters	0.0013	Cubic yards

To convert from degrees Fahrenheit (F) to degrees Celsius (C), first subtract 32, then multiply by $\frac{5}{9}$.

To convert from degrees Celsius to degrees Fahrenheit, multiply by $\frac{9}{5}$, then add 32.

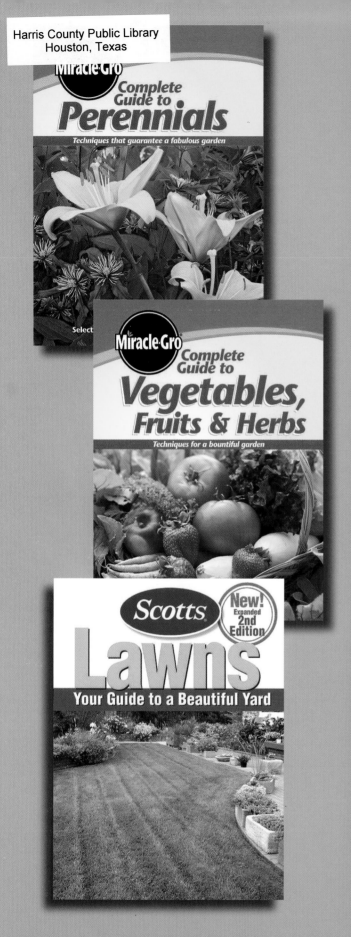

For comprehensive,
in-depth gardening guides,

count on
expert advice
you can trust.

**Pick up these exciting titles
wherever gardening books are sold.**

The brands to trust for all your growing needs

ADT0299_0907